# ACTS OF UNION AND DISUNION

What has held the UK together –
and what is dividing it?

## LINDA COLLEY

P

PROFILE BOOKS

First published in Great Britain in 2014 by
PROFILE BOOKS LTD
3A Exmouth House
Pine Street
London ECIR OJH
*www.profilebooks.com*

By arrangement with the BBC
The BBC logo and Radio 4 logo are a trade mark of the
British Broadcasting Corporation and are used under licence.
Radio 4 © 2014

10 9 8 7 6 5 4 3 2 1

Printed and bound in Great Britain by
CPI Group (UK) Ltd, Croydon, CR0 4YY

Extract from Seamus Heaney's 'Act of Union' used with kind permission of Faber and Faber, from *North* (1975, Faber and Faber).

A CIP catalogue record for this book is available from the British Library.

ISBN 978 1 78125 185 0
eISBN 978 1 78283 013 9

The paper this book is printed on is certified by the © 1996 Forest Stewardship Council A.C. (FSC). It is ancient-forest friendly. The printer holds FSC chain of custody SGS-COC-2061

FSC
www.fsc.org
MIX
Paper from
responsible sources
FSC® C020471

# CONTENTS

In admiring memory of
JOHN MORTON BLUM
(1921–2011)

and

EDMUND SEARS MORGAN
(1916–2013)

Wise Men, Great Friends

A comic map by Frederick W. Rose in 1880, an election year, illustrates the longevity of sharp territorial divisions in the United Kingdom, and how these have often been reinforced and expressed by struggles between its political parties: in this case by the rivalry between Benjamin Disraeli, Lord Beaconsfield, in Tory southern England, and the Liberal William Gladstone in Scotland and the North. Subsequent editions of the map also positioned anti-Disraeli sentiment in Cornwall and Wales.

# PREFACE

Towards the end of 2012, I was commissioned by BBC
Radio 4 to write and deliver a series of talks on acts of
union and disunion, and how they can help us both to
understand and question the British past. The number of
projected episodes soon expanded from ten to fifteen, but
the agreed format involved strict limitations and demands
that proved at once challenging and liberating. Each pro-
gramme was to last no more than fifteen minutes, and my
own spoken words were to be intermixed with snatches
of music, poetry, diaries, biography, novels, drama and
political speeches. From the outset, it was agreed that,
while I would focus on England, Wales, Scotland and
Ireland, and on their divisions and interconnections, the
programmes would also touch on these countries' relations over time with other continents, and with the one-
time British Empire. And while the immediate hooks for
the series were the forthcoming referendum on Scottish
independence and a possible referendum on British with-
drawal from the European Union, it was clear to me that

– in order to be useful and faithful to its subject-matter – *Acts of Union and Disunion* would need to be firmly rooted in the long and deep past. Current events are saturated by comment from the media, on the web, and from the politically involved. Professional historians can and should offer something rather different.

Accordingly, I decided to structure the series around the successive legislative acts of union that served to create the United Kingdom, which meant going back to the sixteenth century, and on occasions to even earlier times. I also wanted to examine some of the wider, international unions and would-be unions in which all or some of these islands have been involved, of which the European Union is only the most recent. And I interpreted 'acts of union' generously, looking not just at specific political *events*, but also at some of the drawn-out *processes* that at different times aided (or compromised) the imagining and workings of the United Kingdom. In particular, I wanted to address some of the constitutive stories of identity that in the past helped to mobilise and bind together some of the peoples of these islands, but which are now for the most part much depleted. Accordingly, the fifteen broadcasts scheduled for January 2014 were very much my personal interpretations of certain selected themes and connected topics, and there was much else I would have liked to include that had to be left out, or that could only be glanced at. This book is an amplified version of these original radio scripts, and contains much additional material; but it follows the same fifteen-part format and pitch, and is again perforce selective in its subject matter.

Addressing a wider than usual audience on these issues in multimedia formats has been a challenge and an opportunity I have much relished, and not just because it has catered to some of my own longstanding intellectual interests. In recent years, the study and worth of the humanities have come under growing pressure and questioning on both sides of the Atlantic. It is therefore all the more important, I firmly believe, for academic historians to reach out to different constituencies, by way of different methods and technologies, and to demonstrate how and why their discipline possesses a value and interest that extend far beyond narrow specialist circles.

But *Acts of Union and Disunion* is not just about the past. Nor, in some of its deeper engagements, is it exclusively concerned with one specific polity. For while much of the book addresses the peculiarities of British and Irish history, and of the United Kingdom in which for a time those histories were conjoined, some of the themes it explores and the dilemmas it charts possess a broader resonance. In recent decades, the United Kingdom has become increasingly exposed to changes and trials that are often lumped together under the heading 'globalisation'. The resurgent angst over identity politics touched on in these pages needs to be understood in part in this light: as reactions in one particular location – the countries of the United Kingdom – to trends such as increasing immigration and erosions of national sovereignty that are being experienced and raged against in many other areas of the world. For all the chatter over Euro-scepticism, the United Kingdom also visibly shares in developments and anxieties that are broadly European. Like many European states (and many states outside Europe), the United Kingdom has had to deal with various stateless national and cultural groupings that in some cases are becoming hungrier for states of their own. This might not pose so many problems if the European Union were indeed what some critics accuse it of being: a mega supra-national state, a new kind of empire in process. If Brussels really were the potent capital of an emerging empire, then not just the new Scotland that may soon come into being, but also – say – a future independent Cornwall, Mercia, Yorkshire, Wales, Basque Country, Corsica, Faroe Islands, Catalonia, Lombardy, Walloon or Sami republic and more might all hope to find secure shelter and a sense of wider belonging under the EU's capacious umbrella.

At present, however, the problem is not so much that the European Union is over-strong, but rather that in many respects it is weak, inchoate and uncertain. Indeed, it is arguable that by trying to forge a currency union so far in advance of anything approaching political union, the EU has put the second and greater aspiration at deep risk and beyond any foreseeable possibility of successful attainment. In these circumstances, and given the existence of great, competing powers such as the United States, China, India and Russia, the further fragmentation of what is already a deeply divided Europe poses enormous challenges in prospect. All of which is to say that, while *Acts of Union and Disunion* focuses on one particular state-nation that is under growing pressure, the following pages develop arguments and themes that possess a wider contemporary relevance.

Because I have needed and wanted to present this material in different ways, I have accumulated more diverse debts than is usual when engaged on a scholarly and creative project. My writing began in London and Norfolk, but it was completed at the Cullman Center for Scholars and Writers at the New York Public Library, which awarded me a Birkelund Fellowship in 2013. I thank the Center's director, Jean Strouse, and her staff, and my fellow Fellows for a wonderfully inspiring and supportive time. At different stages I have received expert advice and specialist guidance from many friends and colleagues, and especially from Nicholas Ashton, David Bell, Huw Bowen, Roy Foster, Melissa Lane, Guy Lodge, Martin Loughlin, Gethin Matthews, Julie Mellby, Sheila O'Connell, Padraic Scanlan and Bob Tignor, while Paris Amanda Spies-Gans has been an inspired and relentlessly active picture researcher. At the BBC, my first contacts were with James Cook and Timothy Prosser, but the series would never have been completed without the professionalism and commitment of Philip Sellars and above all Simon Elmes. At Profile Books, Penny Daniel, Hannah Ross, Cecily Gayford, Trevor Horwood, Drew Jerrison and especially Andrew Franklin expertly and enthusiastically managed the transition of my text from one medium to another. Gill Coleridge, Peter Straus and Cara Jones at Rogers, Coleridge and White were as ever a constant support. So, abundantly, was David Cannadine, to an even greater degree than is usual, tolerating and aiding my absorption both at the laptop and at the microphone.

*Acts of Union and Disunion* is dedicated to the memory of

two great friends and historians, whom I was lucky enough to meet while on the faculty of Yale University. But, as I was completing this project, it occurred to me that I would never have dared to range in such a compressed and audacious fashion over so many subjects had I not had to do much the same in decades of delivering lectures to students first at Cambridge, then at Yale, then at the London School of Economics, and finally now at Princeton University. To those multitudes of men and women on whom I have tried out so many of these arguments and ideas over the years – and who have repeatedly made me think harder and afresh – I also render heartfelt thanks.

LJC
*London, Norfolk, Princeton and New York*

# Part I
# STORIES

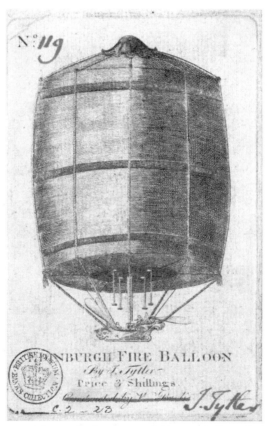

Admission ticket to the first successful hot-air balloon flight over Britain, made by James Tytler above Edinburgh on 27 August 1784.

# 1

# ORIENTATION

At five o'clock on the morning of 27 August 1784, James Tytler became the first person to survey Britain from the skies, sailing 350 feet above the ground in a hot-air balloon of his own design. This brief, unique experience of gazing across distant horizons and of looking down at his fellow men failed to give him either serenity or a sense of Olympian detachment.

Tytler was a Scot, a son of the manse from what is now Angus, and a brilliant, restless, troubled and radical man. Before emigrating to the United States, where he drowned in 1804 under the influence of drink, he kept himself going and funded his inventions by working as an apothecary, and as a hack writer and controversialist. One of his fiercest print controversies was with another Scot, John Pinkerton. Pinkerton was a more comfortably off individual, an Edinburgh antiquarian and poet who devoted several volumes to arguing that the prime credit for peopling and shaping these islands should go to ancient Germanic and Teutonic tribes, to the Saxons. Tytler disagreed. He was prepared to describe the island of Great Britain as 'a nation', but he also believed passionately in the 'antiquity of the Scottish nation', and in the vital importance of the Celts. Pinkerton's theories, Tytler raged, filled 'Britain and Ireland with a kind of mongrel nation ... but this is not sufficient'.

As this quarrel between two eighteenth-century Scots illustrates, there is nothing new about disagreements over the nature, histories and identities of Britain: and its experience is hardly unique in that regard. Virtually every state that has ever existed has contained multiple fault-lines, be they ethnic, religious, linguistic, cultural or territorial differences, or other sources of internal division. Moreover, in the past, as now, many states have been composites. In other words, like China, India, or Spain – or the present United Kingdom – they have been assemblages of different and distinctive countries and territories that were once separately ruled and organised. So the divided nature of these islands is hardly exceptional, and the current disputes over these divisions possess ample precedents. Although 'Britain' is still sometimes viewed as an old and peculiarly stable country, these are selective visions. Historically speaking, Great Britain, and still more the United Kingdom, are comparatively recent and synthetic constructs that have often been contested and in flux in the past, just as they continue to be contested and in flux now.

The first settlers seem to have arrived in Britain some 800,000 years ago, coming by way of the land bridge that connected it then to the Continent. These incomers did not last long, and neither did their immediate successors. Cycles of terrible weather and obliterating ice meant that wave after wave of settlers here was utterly wiped out, and it is probably only in the last 11,500 years that one can talk of British ancestors living on British soil in any continuous way. That means that, in terms of indigenous peoples clinging on and surviving, Britain, and indeed Ireland, possess shorter histories than, say, Australia or America.

But Britain and the United Kingdom are also recent constructs in terms of much shorter-scale history. 'Britain' and 'Great Britain' were occasionally used as collective terms for Wales, Scotland and England in the early medieval era, and some leading political actors and propagandists argued for, and asserted the necessary union of these countries from very early on. In the twelfth century, for instance, a Welsh cleric who was possibly of Breton extraction, Geoffrey of Monmouth, produced a history of the kings of Britain, *Historia Regum Britanniae*. This claimed – with an audacious disregard for evidence – that England, Wales and Scotland had once, in the lost mists of time, 'from sea to sea', been unified under a single monarch, first by the Trojan Brutus, and then by King Arthur himself. It was not until the sixteenth century, however, that the phrase 'Great Britain' became more widely used at official level; and it was only in 1603 that a Scottish king, James VI, united under his single rule the three kingdoms of England and Wales, Scotland and Ireland. Even then, Scotland retained its own parliament until the Act of Union of 1707, while the overarching name 'Great Britain' remained a disputed one. Jonathan Swift, author of *Gulliver's Travels*, hated the concept of Great Britain, in part because it excluded and marginalised his native Ireland. 'I never will call it Britain, pray don't call it Britain,' Swift wrote to his faithful correspondent Stella in 1711. 'Pox on the modern phrase Great Britain,' he wrote over twenty years later: and it is striking that – even in 1738 – Swift still viewed 'Great Britain' as something distinctly *modern*.

'The United Kingdom', as a collective term for England, Wales, Scotland and for all or part of Ireland, is an even more recent invention. It only became the official umbrella designation for all four of these countries in 1801, and not for long. As a result of the Irish revolution which began in 1916, what had formerly been 'The United Kingdom of Great Britain and Ireland' shrank in 1922 to the official term that exists today: 'The United Kingdom of Great Britain and Northern Ireland'.

But the United Kingdom has never proved a very compelling identifying name. No one has ever proudly and seriously referred to himself or herself as a 'UKanian'. And I suspect that few men and women have ever set out bravely to fight and struggle and die explicitly for the *United Kingdom*, even though millions have fought and died over the centuries out of loyalty to Britain, Ireland, Wales, Scotland and England. It is suggestive that in the 2012 London Olympics it was 'Team GB' – Team *Great Britain* – that was chosen as the name for the home team, not 'Team UK', even though the latter would have been more correct. This particular acronym, 'UK', is the most recently invented label for the state we are in. If you go online and check Google's Ngram viewer, you will find that 'UK', as an acronym for the United Kingdom, only seems to have started becoming common in books and newspapers and speeches from about the 1970s.

Why did this come about? Why, in recent decades, have these two letters *UK* acquired such wide currency? Part of the appeal of UK, I suspect – especially for politicians and the media – is that it serves as a kind of euphemism. It is probably the case that a majority of people in England, Wales, Scotland and Northern Ireland are still willing to describe themselves as 'British', at least in some circumstances. But there is now a significant minority in these countries that does not want to describe itself as British in any circumstances: hence the attraction of the more neutral-seeming 'UK', and of other euphemisms such as 'the home nations'.

In recent decades, indeed, the flux, uncertainty and debate that have often characterised Great Britain and the United Kingdom have become more evident and more raw. At one level, this was given official expression in the devolution measures of 1998 and after, with Wales, Scotland and Northern Ireland – but not England – acquiring or consolidating parliaments or quasi-parliaments of their own, existing in tandem with the Westminster Parliament. At another level, and especially since the 1970s, a succession of writers and pundits has predicted a 'break-up of Britain': and such predictions may become justified by events. On 18 September 2014, the people of Scotland will vote on whether their country should secede from the Union established in 1707, and become an independent state.

In this book, I will be discussing not simply the background of these current controversies and divisions, but also and mainly longer histories. I want to examine some of the forces, ideas and initiatives that have served to bring together many (never all) of the people in these islands, especially from the sixteenth century – or at least allowed many (never all) of them for some of the time peacefully to coexist. Conversely, I also want to explore some of the influences that have made for divisions between England, Wales, Scotland and Ireland, and also for fractures within these countries. *Acts of Union and Disunion* is not – and I manifestly do not intend it as – a comprehensive history of what is now (shall we call it?) the UK. The essays in this book, like the radio broadcasts on which it is based, are rather one historian's perspectives on a selection of connected themes. Given how controversial some of these are, and the compression my format dictates, some readers may well find themselves at times in disagreement. So it is right that I should say something about myself and my background.

I am what the balloonist James Tytler might have styled a mongrel. My mother's parents were Welsh. My father was born in Shrewsbury, near the border between England and Wales. There is Irishness in my family background. I grew up in the north of England. And, since the early 1980s, I have spent most of my career working as a historian in universities on the east coast of the United States, first at Yale, named after Elihu Yale whose family came from Denbighshire, and now at Princeton in New Jersey, which was founded in 1746 by Scots-Irish Presbyterians. In part because of my interest in Britain's imperial diaspora, I have also spent time in regions of Australia and India, in some Caribbean and African countries, in Hong Kong and Singapore, and in parts of the Mediterranean world: Gibraltar, Menorca and Malta. In all of these places, and in many more, there were people in the past, of widely different ethnic, religious and cultural backgrounds, who were prepared nonetheless to describe themselves as British subjects, or even simply as British.

I will be touching on some of these one-time British imperial spaces and connections in later essays, and I will also be situating the 'home islands' throughout in even wider international contexts. Because, whatever your position on the United Kingdom and its various component parts, these territories cannot be understood in isolation. Nor can some of their problems and characteristics be understood in isolation. There has never been a substantial politically defined population anywhere on the globe that has been natural or primordial. All countries are synthetic and imperfect creations and subject to change, and most have been the result of violent conflict at some stage. That said, composite states such as the United Kingdom – what some political scientists have termed 'state-nations' – confront particular challenges. Whereas full-blown nation-states have often sought straightforwardly to assimilate, enforcing a single language, say, or seeking to propagate through compulsory schooling a dominant understanding of the national past, or deliberately stamping out emblems and expressions of difference, state-nations have to operate on at least two levels. Their leaders have to acknowledge and protect the partial autonomy and separate rights and cultures of the various countries and regions that are contained within the state-nation. Simultaneously, they have to create and sustain and nurture a sense of belonging and allegiance with regard to the larger political community. In successful state-nations, there has ideally to be a well thought-out and steady commitment to the whole – and a vision of what that is – as well as recognition of and concessions to the component parts. Arguably, it has been a growing failure since the Second World War to keep renovated this kind of two-level strategy, creative attention to the whole as well as to the parts, that lies behind some of the United Kingdom's current dissensions.

Looking at the span of human history, it is indeed not so much the break-up of some states and nations that is remarkable, but rather the degree to which some of them have managed – at least for a time – to persist and cohere. In order to persist and cohere, states usually require effective political institutions, a degree of material well-being, efficient means of defence against external enemies, mechanisms for maintaining internal order and, very often, some kind of religious or ideological underpinning. In addition, political peoples who manage to cohere usually evolve, foster and substantially believe stories about themselves. In order to succeed and flourish, states and nations need an attractive idea of what they are. So what have been the stories of identity, union and belonging that varieties of Britons have selected to foster and tell about themselves? That is what I now want to discuss.

# ISLANDS

States and nations often develop and deploy stories to do with their real or imagined geography. The French have traditionally imagined their country's frontiers (which in reality have often been in flux) as making up a hexagon, while many Americans believe that it was manifest destiny that allowed them to stretch across a continent from sea to shining sea. For varieties of Britons, the most productive theme for geographical stories has always been islandhood.

> This royal throne of kings, this scepter'd isle,
> This earth of majesty, this seat of Mars,
> This other Eden, demi-paradise,
> This fortress, built by Nature for herself,
> Against infection and the hand of war;
> This happy breed of men, this little world;
> This precious stone set in the silver sea,
> Which serves it in the office of a wall,
> Or as a moat defensive to a house, against the
>     envy of less happier lands,

> This blessed plot, this earth, this realm, this
> England.

Put into the mouth of John of Gaunt in Act 2 of *Richard II*, these are some of Shakespeare's most famous lines. Over the centuries, hundreds of other writers have drawn inspiration from them, not least a Scottish author named Henrietta Elizabeth Marshall. In 1905, Marshall published *Our Island Story*, a children's history book which begins with a fable about Neptune, god of the sea, selecting Britain as his special island. Recently re-issued, *Our Island Story* was, so he claims, a particular favourite of David Cameron when he was young. That the current British prime minister, also of Scottish ancestry, should choose to publicise his early commitment to stories of islandhood is revealing. Yet these island identity tales are not as straightforward as they may appear.

Consider that speech by John of Gaunt more closely.

The real John of Gaunt was so named because he was born, in 1340, in the Belgian town of Ghent, some thirty miles from Brussels. Moreover, *Richard II* is hardly a work of confident national assertion, but rather a play that is crucially about civil war and the murder of a king. So while Shakespeare certainly makes his John of Gaunt speak patriotism, he also makes him minatory and sombre. This scepter'd isle, this blessed plot, this precious stone is also – it is made clear – insecure and embattled. It requires a moat to guard it against war and infection. Gaunt's speech can be misleading in another respect. In geographical fact, this England is not a scepter'd isle, or any other kind of isle. It is rather the largest portion of an island that contains two other countries, Wales and Scotland, and that is also part of a numerous and variegated archipelago.

There are over 6,000 other islands around the island of Great Britain. One of them – the island of Ireland – is large, almost 33,000 square miles. But many of these islands are tiny, like most of the 500 islands of the Hebrides, and some are quasi-autonomous. The Isle of Man came under the full sovereignty of the British monarch only in 1765 and retains its own parliament, while Orkney and the Shetlands were once linked to Scandinavia. It has never simply been a case, then, of what Winston Churchill styled 'our long island history'. There are multiple islands involved in the British past, with multiple and sometimes diverging histories. The notion of 'our island story' is misleading and inadequate in other ways too. For most of the last million years, what is now Great Britain was not an island at all. Even when the land bridge that once joined it to the rest of Europe melted away, Continental connections persisted. From the early Middle Ages until the nineteenth century, a succession of monarchs based in the island of Britain also ruled parts of Continental Europe. Even now, the United Kingdom possesses a tiny, prosperous Continental European outpost in Gibraltar.

But geographical stories and myths of identity do not need to be entirely accurate in order to be influential. In reality, it was not manifest destiny or even just democratic ideals that allowed the United States to span a 3000-mile wide continent, but land-hungry settlers, systems of slavery, a great deal of warfare and imperialism, and a measure of genocide. Moreover, in the 1860s, the US erupted into civil war and came close to fragmenting. Nonetheless, the idea of a manifest and relentless territorial destiny remains immensely attractive among all sorts of Americans. By the same token, ideas and myths of islandhood have proved persistent and seductive in Britain, in part because they have served multiple purposes.

Most obviously, invoking islandhood – with its seemingly clear and all-encompassing physical limits – has catered to those wanting political union in Great Britain, or at least peaceful coexistence between its component parts. 'It is an unnatural thing that war should be fought between us,' insisted a Scottish envoy to England in 1484, 'we who are bound together within a small island in the western sea.' When James VI of Scotland inherited in addition the throne of England in 1603, he too argued that geography had preordained political union. God had 'made us all in one island', he reminded his new, somewhat sceptical English subjects, 'compassed with one sea'. Over a century later, another ardent champion of British union, Daniel Defoe, also invoked the instrumentality of islandhood in the title of a famous travel book. First published in the mid 1720s, Defoe's celebratory *Tour thro' the whole island of Great Britain* remained a bestseller for over fifty years and is still in print.

Defoe, of course, was also obsessed with islandhood in his fictional writings. Like Robert Louis Stevenson's *Treasure Island*, or H. G. Wells's *Island of Dr Moreau*, or George Bernard Shaw's play, *John Bull's Other Island*, or Thomas More's island of Utopia, Defoe's great novel *Robinson*

*Crusoe* (1719) demonstrates how strongly island motifs have inflected culture here, and not just politics. The experiences and reactions that Defoe gives his eponymous hero underline the point that island references serve multiple purposes. Robinson Crusoe's desert island is sequentially a place of fear and confinement, a location of solitary achievement and religious contemplation, and ultimately a site of empire, a colony. Much the same has proved the case in real British life. Over the centuries, varieties of Britons have used island motifs to express anxiety, as ways to proclaim and explore distinctiveness, and in order to help make sense of empire.

As in *Richard II*, allusions to islandhood have often signalled vulnerability, and for good reasons. When Shakespeare wrote this play in the 1590s the reigning monarch, Elizabeth I, was old and possessed no direct heir, which meant that no one could feel confident that the civil wars of the past might not break out again, as they duly did in the 1640s. There were external dangers, too, in the form of great Continental powers such as Spain, France and, ultimately, Germany, that possessed bigger land forces than Britain did itself. When war and invasion threatened, imagining Britain as a 'right little, tight little island' – to quote from a song composed during the Napoleonic Wars – could be a way of expressing fear at being besieged and at risk. But invoking islandhood might instead administer comfort, as with Vera Lynn's 1942 recording of 'The White Cliffs of Dover'. And islandhood could serve as a metaphor for heroic defiance. Think again of the Second World War, and of the famous – perhaps too famous – cartoon

A Second World War propaganda poster by Donald Blake shows the United Kingdom, a clearly demarcated site of busy industry, launching attacks by air and sea against the Continent.

by David Low, a New Zealander of Scottish descent. Published in London in 1940, it shows a solitary soldier standing on the rocky shoreline of Britain, raising a fist at an approaching swarm of Luftwaffe bombers, and crying out 'Very well, alone!'

There was another important respect in which islandhood expressed simultaneously a sense of being beleaguered and the conviction of being special. Historians disagree over how quickly the Protestant Reformation swept through England, Wales and Scotland. Certainly, it never succeeded totally in any of these countries, and it substantially failed in Ireland. Nonetheless, Britain was often represented – in hymns, secular music, art, literature, journalism, sermons and political speeches – as a distinctively Protestant island. Even the Irish Protestant minority sometimes viewed itself as a kind of virtual, virtuous island holding out in a land that was overwhelmingly populated by Catholics.

Assertions of blessed Protestant insularity remained widespread far into the twentieth century. Their effects were often malign, and not just in Ireland. I remember an elderly lady telling me how – as a young child and along with many others – she was evacuated during the Second World War to deepest Wales. On arrival, the other children were quickly whisked off by their host families, but for a long while she was left alone on the station platform and no one would take her. Why? Because a label around her neck made it clear that she was a Catholic, and this part of Wales was a bastion of Protestant nonconformity. Yet if Protestant zeal sometimes sowed prejudice and cruel division, it could also foster powerful ideas of national cohesion. As the librettos of Handel's oratorios demonstrate, Britain could be imagined as the Protestant Israel, God's very own chosen island. A black immigrant to Britain during the eighteenth century took note of these ideas, and when he came to publish his autobiography was careful to play on them. 'I imagined', he wrote, 'that all the inhabitants of this island were holy.'

This conviction of being God's chosen islanders undoubtedly fed into British imperialism, with its marked and confident sense of mission, and its frequent aggression and racial arrogance. There was a sense indeed in which the empire served to multiply Britain's own island stories and render them a worldwide phenomenon. A large part of the British Empire was, after all, made up of islands: Jamaica, Barbados, Bermuda, Trinidad, Bombay, Hong Kong, Singapore, New Zealand, Newfoundland, Malta, Ceylon, St Helena where the British imprisoned Napoleon, and the Falkland Islands, where they fought their last successful twentieth-century war. Even the vast terrain of Australia seems quickly to have been seen in insular terms. 'They go to an Island to take special charge', wrote a balladeer in 1786 of the first convict fleet then getting ready to set sail to Botany Bay: 'Much warmer than Britain, and ten times as large'.

This balladeer's geographical knowledge was evidently limited. Australia is over thirty times bigger than Britain. Nonetheless, his lines alert us to some important paradoxes about British stories of islandhood. Those aboard the eleven ships of the First Fleet were mostly convicts, male

*Treasure Island*, painting by Daniel Boyd (Kudjla/Gangalu peoples), 2005. An aboriginal artist's perspective on colonists' greed and on the notion that Australia was 'empty' before their invasions, showing its many ancient indigenous language groups.

and female, being sent to Botany Bay as punishment. But very large numbers of English, Welsh, Irish and Scottish men and women would subsequently choose to emigrate to Australia and other British settlement colonies, and to the lost empire of the United States and elsewhere in the world. Islands, as Robinson Crusoe discovered, can be confining, restrictive places. And over the centuries, strikingly large numbers of miscellaneous Britons have selected to turn their back on their home's island stories and have gone somewhere else.

As this suggests, stories of islandhood by no means always made for insularity. Indeed, British islandhood almost invariably served to promote both inward and outward mobility and contact with others. The sea has not been a moat or a barrier. It has been a bridge.

Frontispiece to *The Naval History of Britain* (London, 1756).
Note the element of invention, with Neptune indicating that
Britain's naval glory stretches back to Alfred the Great.

# 3

# SEA

We do not usually associate the British Isles with conspicuous geographical size, but – in terms of its seaboard – this is a big archipelago. There are over 11,000 miles of coastline around Great Britain, and another 2000 miles around Ireland. There are also thousands of offshore islands. So while the coast of mainland Scotland stretches for over 4000 miles, this total almost trebles if you include some of its larger islands: the Orkneys, Shetland, and the Arran and Western Isles. All of which is to say that coastal living, coastal working and coastal watching have been major parts of experience and culture here. So, emphatically, has the sea, though in different ways, at different times.

The most celebrated and ritualistic assertion of the sea's Britannic importance occurs now on the last night of the BBC's annual promenade concerts, aired on both television and radio:

> When Britain first at heaven's command,
> Arose from out the azure main,

This was the charter of the land.
And guardian angels sang this strain:

'Rule, Britannia! Britannia rule the waves!
Britons never, never, never shall be slaves.'

'The nations not so blest as thee
Must, in their turn, to tyrants fall,
While thou shalt flourish great and free:
The dread and envy of them all.'

The joint creation of an English Catholic composer, Thomas Arne, and a Scottish Presbyterian poet and playwright, James Thomson, 'Rule, Britannia!' was first performed in 1740, but the ideas behind it were older. From the late sixteenth century, a succession of politicians, propagandists and scholars, such as the Welsh mathematician and alchemist John Dee, had drawn on maritime references in order to manufacture claims about Britain's special destiny. The encircling seas, it was argued, demonstrated that God and Nature had designed Britain as a single polity, and had also provided for it a distinctive mission and medium. 'We seem ... to have been formed by Providence', remarked one writer, 'for ploughing the sea'. In these flattering visions, the sea became a blank canvas for future British enterprise and, indeed, for future British expansion. 'All thine shall be the subject main', predicts Thomson glowingly in 'Rule, Britannia!': 'And every shore it circles thine'.

Yet, before the 1600s, the various rulers of these islands generally lacked the monetary and political resources to build up and maintain effective navies. As a result, the lengthy coastlines of the British archipelago proved constantly vulnerable to sea raiders and to invasions, and not just by Romans, Vikings, Saxons, Normans and other early incomers. Even though by the mid seventeenth century the Royal Navy was beginning to develop serious strength, it still failed to prevent the last major foreign invasion of these shores – an event that happened not in 1066, but in 1688. The invader this time was William, Prince of Orange, the formidable and profoundly Calvinist ruler of the Dutch republic. In some of the patriotic history books that I was made to read as a child, William featured unequivocally as a liberator who landed at Torbay in Devon on 5 November 1688 strictly by invitation. In cold reality, William arrived after much planning and expensive preparation, equipped with some 500 ships and over 21,000 Dutch, German and Scandinavian troops. So the English had limited choice in the matter. Neither did many Scots or Irish have much choice when William's forces moved on to them.

By the time 'Rule, Britannia!' came to be written, the situation had substantially altered. By the 1740s, the Royal Navy was fast becoming the most powerful on the world's oceans, blocking almost all later invasion attempts, keeping sea routes open for Britain's expanding mercantile marine, and ruthlessly fostering and abetting empire. Amnesia now substantially descended about the maritime failings and defeats of the past, and it began to be asserted and widely believed that Britain had *always* exercised dominion over the waves, and that doing so was its peculiar right and genius.

Drawing analogies between a ship at sea and the organisation of a state had been customary since classical times. Now, as the Royal Navy peaked in power, it came to be widely represented and viewed as an emblem and metaphor for Britain itself, its increasing victories and reach an expression and embodiment of national virility. Navy ships were treated as physical extensions of Britain. So, if a child happened to be born on a Royal Navy vessel – not an impossible event since women sometimes defied the rules and went to sea – then, irrespective of its parentage, it immediately acquired by law the right to be a British subject. The amalgamation of the fighting navy at sea and British identities on land became still more pronounced in the early twentieth century, when the practice began of naming large numbers of ships after towns and regions of the United Kingdom. Only think of some of the ships that were destroyed and damaged during the Falklands War in 1982. Their names echo almost eerily the four component parts of the present United Kingdom: HMS *Antrim* for Northern Ireland, HMS *Glamorgan* for Wales, HMS *Glasgow* for Scotland, and HMS *Sheffield* and HMS *Coventry* for England.

But the pull and significance of the sea rested on more than the Royal Navy. A disproportionate number of major British and Irish towns and cities are situated on or near the coast. In Scotland, for instance, Glasgow, Edinburgh, Dundee and Aberdeen all have their own or adjacent seaports. Until the 1960s, and the slow decline of British seaside resorts, domestic coastlines were major sites for leisure and pleasure. Until the railway network was well established, going by ship was usually the fastest means of getting around Great Britain, and – before the aeroplane – manifestly the only form of travel between Britain and Ireland. And the sea was a major civilian employer, not just in the mercantile marine, but also in fishing, forestry and carpentry, sail making, brewing, engineering, rope making, victualling, coal and iron ore mining, and above all shipbuilding. By 1911, the UK was producing almost 70 per cent of the world's seagoing vessels; and massive shipyards on the Clyde, in Cardiff, Belfast, London, Southampton, Newcastle on Tyne and Liverpool welded together the different component parts of these islands in a common industrial enterprise.

At one level, these civilian connections to the sea straightforwardly increased its utility as a constitutive national story. As late as 1959, a government report could describe 'The ubiquity of British shipping' as 'a world wide advertisement for British industry and commerce, and for things British generally'. Yet even when Britain's naval and maritime reach was at its height, the sea was much more than a setting for the willed and conscious enterprise of its own inhabitants. Being interpenetrated by the sea, to paraphrase Joseph Conrad, also resulted in persistent and often involuntary exposure to changes, influences and incomers from without.

The global scale of British maritime trade made precociously possible the import of goods and commodities from other continents that altered lifestyles, ideas and patterns of behaviour very widely: tea, cotton, coffee, tobacco, sugar, porcelain. Whenever you see a portrait of a late seventeenth- or eighteenth-century English, Welsh, Irish or

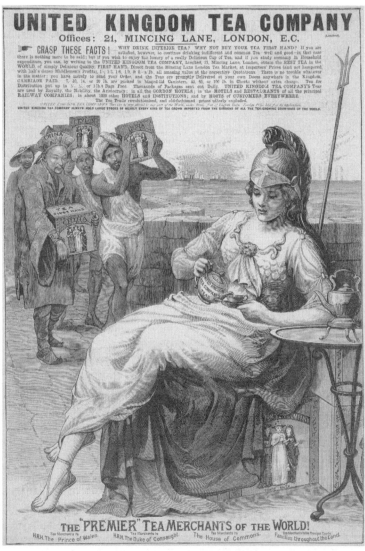

An advertisement in *The Illustrated London News* in 1893
shows an arrogant and lolling Britannia commanding the
world's commodities but also dependent on them.

Scottish man or woman wearing a black, shiny wig, consider that the original hair involved may well have been shipped in from China or other parts of Asia, courtesy of Britain's East India Company. The sea brought in people from other continents too, making the populations of these islands more diverse. The arrival of the *Empire Windrush* at Tilbury docks in June 1948, bearing Polish refugees and almost 500 Jamaicans, is a famous moment in the history of post-war British immigration. But non-European incomers to these islands go back a very long way, and many of them not only arrived by sea, but were also connected in some way to maritime pursuits and industries.

By 1750, London may already have possessed the largest black population of any city in Europe, and almost half of these incomers – who were overwhelmingly male – seem to have worked in the Thames dockyards or in the mercantile marine. Or they were men who had previously been attached to the Royal Navy, like Olaudah Equiano, who first arrived in London in the late 1750s during the Seven Years War, evolved into a fierce opponent of slavery and became the first black writer to publish a bestseller in the English language under his own name. Chinese and Indian sailors also settled in London from the 1700s and, as trade and empire expanded, this sort of cosmopolitan work force increasingly characterised other ports in Britain and Ireland. By 1911, Cardiff was the biggest exporter of coal anywhere on the globe, and it was also a city where half the population came from somewhere else, not just from other parts of Europe and the UK, but also from the West Indies, China, Central America and East Africa.

So while the encircling sea has often featured in books, newspapers, verse, sermons, songs, art and political speeches as a secure marker and buttress of identity, and as a barrier protecting these islands from the medley of the outside world, its long-term impact and influences were in reality mixed, invasive and variable. Some individuals, though, clung fast to the traditional myths and stories and found it hard to let them go. During the massive Empire Exhibition held at Wembley in 1924, when Britain's naval power was already in relative decline, a Welsh historian and geographer named Sir Charles Lucas still felt it appropriate to assert Britain's unique and mutual relationship with the maritime: 'Most of all', he wrote wistfully, 'the old country is loved of the sea.' Lucas was a more subtle man than these words may suggest, acutely aware of some of the political changes that were ongoing in the empire and beyond, and receptive to ideas of racial equality. But, in the wake of 'the latest and greatest chapter in our history', the First World War, he desperately wanted to believe that 'the call has come to the seagoing race to adventure once more upon the stormy seas of time', and that there would be no shipwreck. Not until the 1970s was it generally accepted that the Royal Navy and the merchant fleet were in irreversible decline, and recognised that mass air travel was fundamentally altering how Britons (and everyone else) viewed the sea.

Yet the sea, and stories founded on the sea, continue to have political repercussions here. The discovery of oil and gas in the North Sea in the last third of the twentieth century has done more than convert Aberdeen into a kind of mini-Houston, and enrich towns such as Dundee, Montrose and Leith. It has also allowed nationalists to argue with much greater cogency than before that an independent Scotland could be economically viable. Recently, however, some residents of the Orkney and Shetland Islands have been arguing that some of the richest reserves of oil and gas are actually in *their* stretches of sea, and that it is they – and not mainland Scotland – who should therefore reap the economic benefit, and perhaps even strike out politically on their own. This controversy, which is still ongoing, is yet another example of how the maritime has interpenetrated arguments about identity in these islands. It is also a reminder that James Thomson got it wrong. The sea is subject to no one and to no single power for very long.

BRITISH TREE OF TRUE LIBERTY.

*STABILISSIMUS.*

A conservative view of British 'true liberty', representing it as rooted in
the existing constitution and religion, and as productive of happiness.

# 4

# LIBERTY

On 20 April 1964, Nelson Mandela delivered what was to be his last formal speech for twenty-seven years. On trial for his life at Pretoria's Palace of Justice, and speaking from the dock, he deliberately set out some of the British roots of his opposition to South Africa's system of apartheid. Although Marxist critics had sometimes viewed Western parliamentary systems as reactionary, remarked Mandela, he himself was an:

> admirer of such a system. The Magna Carta, the Petition of Rights, and the Bill of Rights are documents which are held in veneration by democrats throughout the world. I have great respect for British political institutions, and for the country's system of justice. I regard the British Parliament as the most democratic institution in the world, and the independence and impartiality of its judiciary never fail to arouse my admiration.

Mandela's reasons for speaking in these terms were partly tactical: to underline that his thinking had been influenced 'by both West and East', and to draw in some of his white supporters. Yet this was by no means the only time that an opponent of British imperialism chose nonetheless to celebrate British freedoms. A Virginian named Patrick Henry who had fought against the British during the American Revolution was just as flattering in 1788. Addressing the Virginian Convention gathered to approve the draft of the new US constitution, Henry reminded its delegates of 'Our glorious forefathers of Great Britain [who] made liberty the foundation of every thing. That country is become a great, mighty, and splendid nation ... because liberty is its direct end and foundation.' It was another participant in the American Revolution, however, who offered the most moving celebration of British liberty. One of thousands of black slaves to escape from their American owners so as to throw in their lot with the British, this man signalled his new allegiance by changing his name. Even though he may well have been shipped to America by British slave traders, he chose to rename himself 'British freedom'.

These testimonies by individuals who had experienced some of the harsher dimensions of British power indicate how significant a part stories concerning liberty have played in Britons' sense of identity – *and* in their projection of themselves and their polity to others. These same testimonies also alert us to some of the ambiguities of these liberty stories. During the eighteenth century, Britain probably shipped more Africans into slavery than any other European power. And from the 1760s to the mid twentieth century, Britain laid claim to the world's biggest empire. So what exactly was the quality of this celebrated British liberty?

As a cult and mode of memory, it rested in part on bad history, especially bad *English* history. As early as the thirteenth century arguments were being put forward that before the Norman Conquest in 1066, England had been a uniquely free country equipped with advanced self-governing institutions. Although suppressed by the Normans, these ancient freedoms, it was contended, remained in the national bloodstream, as it were, always awaiting rediscovery and revived expression. Such notions proved immensely valuable to generations of radicals, and not just in England. Claiming that a particular innovation or reform was in fact an ancient right, one that had existed before the Norman Yoke and which now needed to be restored, became a widespread and persistent tactic for advancing and sanctioning demands for change. Take the case of Joseph Gerrald, who was part Irish, born in St Kitts in 1763, and put on trial for sedition in Edinburgh in 1794 for supporting universal male suffrage. Gerrald took his stand not on the radicalism of these demands, but on what he represented as customary rights: 'Among the records of former times, and in the established usages of our ancestors', he argued, 'we sought for precedent, and we found it.' It was 'our Saxon ancestors which gave us freedom', he assured the Scottish High Court of Judiciary, adding, 'You are Britons – you are freemen.' Later advocates of women's suffrage sometimes employed this same tactic of citing supposedly ancient native precedents in order to push for what were novel freedoms in fact. 'Be wise, be fair, be just, *be British*', declared a Suffragettes' poster in 1913: 'and ask your Members of Parliament to vote for Women's Suffrage.'

Supporting such imaginings of a liberty-drenched ancient past were some real and important laws and texts: the Petition of Right of 1628, for instance, which imposed restrictions on royal power, the Habeas Corpus Act of 1679, and the Bill of Rights of 1689, a phrase and concept which the Americans borrowed when they adopted their own Bill of Rights in 1791. But the most important text, first in English and then increasingly in British constitutive stories of liberty, was Magna Carta.

This was wrested from King John by his barons in 1215 and catered to their sectional interests. Nonetheless, Magna Carta seems to have been a more ambitious attempt to curb royal authority than analogous documents produced in other early medieval European kingdoms, and it contained evocative phrases such as 'free man'. Moreover, most people – in the past as now – never actually read the original text or its successor versions, so Magna Carta was able to become an infinitely adaptable political totem and standard. John Bradshaw, chief judge of the High Court of Justice that tried Charles I, invoked the 'Great Old Charter' when sentencing the king to death in 1649. The Reform Act of 1832, which reconfigured and amended the UK's representative system, was widely represented – by supporters, artists and writers – as a new 'Great Charter, in which our rights are inscribed in terms never to be erased'. Some Victorian writers indeed argued that Magna Carta was the world's first written constitution. Runnymede, the stretch of land in Surrey where the original text was probably sealed, and which also possessed popular associations with Anglo Saxon constitutionalism, became such a sacred patriotic site that the National Trust assumed control of it in 1929.

But the uses and resonance of Magna Carta were never simply domestic. Allusions to it as a document, and as a founding moment in the progress of human liberty, have been regularly employed to interpret and embellish British interventions overseas. Thus in 1833, when Westminster belatedly passed legislation providing for the phasing out of slavery in the British Empire, this was promptly redescribed and glorified as a 'Magna Carta for negro rights'. And in January 1946 a British diplomat in the United States, John Balfour – a Scot – sought to take credit for the recently signed Charter of the United Nations by styling its preamble as only the most recent of Magna Carta's 'authentic offspring'. The United Kingdom, Balfour went on, possessed a lineage of freedom 'without equal in human history'.

As all this suggests, while liberty has provided a broadly accessible and multiform master narrative whereby varieties of Britons over the centuries have been able to tell and organise stories about themselves and their state, the political repercussions of this have been decidedly mixed. At one level, radicals and reformers in these islands have often invoked ancient liberties, real and imagined, in order to campaign for *new* freedoms. At another level, references to the country's proud heritage of freedom have frequently been drawn on to characterise and legitimise British interventions overseas. In addition, a cult of superior British liberty has often been deployed to uphold and maintain the political status quo at home.

Especially in the wake of the civil wars of the seventeenth century, British politicians and propagandists worked very hard to promote a version of liberty that would be fully compatible with property, hierarchy, order and law-abiding moderation. 'Various have been the significations … that have been given to the word liberty,' advised one guide to British liberties in 1767. 'It does not consist in an unrestrained freedom,' cautioned the author, paraphrasing Montesquieu: 'No.' The British political system was indeed the freest in the world, it was contended, but this meant a commitment to compromise and balance. The argument went like this. Some foreign states – such as pre-revolutionary France, or the Ottoman, Russian and Chinese empires – were absolutist and susceptible to tyranny. Others – such as post-revolutionary France, or the United States – were vulnerable to the vagaries of mass politics, demagoguery and instability. But Britain, with its monarchy, its House of Lords representing aristocracy, and its House of Commons exemplifying the virtues of responsible democracy, had achieved a uniquely happy medium. It was at once 'the firmest and freest form of government upon earth', wrote one contented commentator. Or as the poet Tennyson wrote carefully, Britain was the land that 'sober-suited Freedom chose':

> ... A land of settled government,
> A land of just and old renown,
> Where freedom broadens slowly down
> From precedent to precedent.

By the same token, the language of liberty was drawn on in order to support the British Union. To be sure, Scottish, Irish and Welsh nationalists have often attacked the power of London in the name of freedom, and with their own iconic texts. By the twentieth century – though apparently not before – the Scottish Declaration of Arbroath (1320) was sometimes being explicitly represented and characterised as a declaration of Scottish independence. But the cult of superior and unique British liberty was so powerful and so elastic that for a long time it operated as a cross-border cement and language in common.

One example of this is how people chose to present and interpret tales of William Wallace, the Scottish military leader who fought the English in the thirteenth century, and who was gruesomely executed in London in 1305. Especially since Mel Gibson's film *Braveheart* in 1995, accounts of Wallace's exploits have come to seem straightforwardly anti-English, an unmitigated spur to Scottish nationalism. But this was not how many nineteenth- and early twentieth-century Scots and English seem to have viewed things. Wallace has always been a Scottish patriot hero. But, in the nineteenth century, he was also and crucially viewed as a fighter for liberty, *and therefore as a figure who could easily be celebrated in England as well as in Scotland*. Some Victorians, indeed, chose to view Wallace as a kind of precursor of what was to become a joint *British* commitment to liberty. In 1820 a play based on Wallace's career proved a marked theatrical success at Covent Garden in London, while in 1885 the English popular novelist G. A. Henty published a bestseller about Wallace indicatively entitled *In Freedom's Cause*.

There are, of course, far worse themes around which to wind constitutive stories of identity than freedom and liberty. And it is clear, I think, that had there not seemed some substance to these liberty stories in wide British experience, they would never have remained so powerful for so long. Nonetheless, liberty stories have imposed their own blinkers. Rather like Americans, varieties of Britons have sometimes wanted or been predisposed to believe that – on account of their own pristine freedoms – invading and interfering with other peoples must be for *their* benefit. A prevailing cult of British liberty has sometimes made for domestic blinkers, too, and not just in regard to Ireland.

After the 1832 Reform Act, a higher proportion of the male population in Britain (though again not in Ireland) became enfranchised than in almost any other European state. But after 1850, the United Kingdom increasingly lagged behind other parts of Europe, the United States, and even some of its own colonial dominions in the access it afforded to the franchise. By the start of the twentieth century, the UK franchise was one of the narrowest in Europe. Almost half of Glasgow's male population, for instance, was unable to vote. Far from witnessing distinctive progress towards an ever-brighter liberty, as far as voting rights were concerned, the UK's record was – for a long time – decidedly unimpressive by Western standards. As we commemorate the centenary of the First World War, it is worth remembering that a large proportion of the English, Welsh, Scottish and Irish other ranks who volunteered to fight in 1914 would never have had any direct experience of exercising democratic rights. Believing firmly that they were fighting for freedom, many of them went to the Front without ever having voted for or against the politicians who sent them there.

# 5

# MONARCHY

British official language identifies monarchy as the most vital act of union, and as an enduring one. The very name of this state, 'The United *Kingdom*', makes clear the centrality of the Crown, and conveys a sense of permanence. The national anthem, too, focuses on the Crown and underlines its endurance. It calls on God to save the Queen, and urges: '*Long* live our noble Queen', '*Long* to reign over us', '*Long* may she reign'.

In his famous commentary on the constitution, the Victorian journalist Walter Bagehot offered a detached, even sardonic analysis of the monarchy, but he accepted that the institution was a resilient one. Monarchy, Bagehot suggested, benefited from being a relatively easy political system for people to understand. And the appeal of a royal family of the British type was particularly tenacious, he argued, because it virtually guaranteed 'nice and pretty events' at regular intervals, and held up a glamorous mirror to emotions and choices that were widely shared and familiar. 'A princely marriage', wrote Bagehot, was 'the brilliant edition of a universal fact, and, as such, it rivets mankind'. As we were reminded in July 2013, exactly the same holds true for a princely birth.

Yet Bagehot also recognised that it was inappropriate to place too much stress on royal continuities. Privately, he believed that support for the monarchy might well decline as access to education in the UK became more widespread, and he speculated that such a falling away of support was likely to happen sooner in Scotland than in England. Whatever you think of this, in one respect Bagehot got it right. To understand how and why monarchy has mattered here, one needs to look not just at tradition and custom, but also at disjunctions and at change over time. Let me offer some ruthlessly compressed history to illustrate this point.

A patchwork of different kingdoms existed throughout these islands from the early Middle Ages. Most historians agree that England became a single kingdom during the tenth century, while a single king was able to control most of Scotland with some security by the thirteenth century. Wales and Ireland, however, were more fragmented and conflict-ridden, experiencing multiple and competing rulers. One relic of Ireland's early kings may be the Stone of Scone – or stone of destiny – infamously seized by the English from Gowrie in what is now Perth and Kinross in 1296, installed in Westminster Abbey, and not returned to Scotland till 1996. If the Stone of Scone really is an authentic ancient coronation stone once used by Scottish kings (and opinions differ), it may have been purloined even earlier. Some scholars believe that a Scottish prince 'borrowed' the stone from the Irish high king at Tara in the sixth century, and somehow failed to return it. And though successive English kings tried to conquer the outer zones of the British Isles (hence the symbolic theft of the Stone of Scone) it was in fact a Scottish king – James VI – who finally effected a Union of Crowns, bringing under his single rule in 1603 his own kingdom, Scotland, the kingdoms of Ireland and England, and the principality of Wales.

In the short term, this Union of Crowns produced neither royal stability nor unity. In 1649 James's son and successor, Charles I, was executed in public and Britain became briefly a republic. Monarchy returned in 1660; but in 1688 a grandson and namesake of James was driven off the throne, to be replaced by a Dutch prince William of Orange and his wife, Mary. There was another change of dynasty in 1714, when the English-born Queen Anne died without direct heirs, and was replaced by George of Hanover, a German prince.

As all this suggests, the apparent antiquity of monarchy in these islands masks considerable discontinuities in terms of evolution and the dynasties involved. Moreover, while monarchy has often functioned as a *national* cement and emblem, it has also served to connect all or sections of these islands with other parts of the world. The British Empire, for instance, pivoted ideologically and organisationally on the monarchy. In legal theory, anyone born in the British monarch's dominions anywhere in the world – regardless of religion, race or ancestry – was potentially a British subject, who owed the monarch allegiance and was owed protection in return. 'The King makes no distinction', declared one colonial administrator in 1789, with the bored resignation of someone uttering a commonplace, 'between a man born in Canada and one born in Middlesex: we are all His Majesty's subjects.' The present Queen's position as head of the Commonwealth is in part a pale survival of this previous system and theory of empire-wide British subjecthood.

At intervals, monarchy has also linked some or all of the British Isles politically with parts of Continental Europe. Many medieval 'English' kings also ruled parts of what is now France. After 1688, Britain was linked through its dual monarchs, William of Orange and Queen Mary, to the Dutch republic, sharing politicians, foreign policy, knowledge, print culture, and banking practices with it, as well as rulers. And from 1714, and under four successive King Georges, Britain was linked to Hanover in northern Germany.

This German connection, which at times had a major influence on British government, foreign policy and culture, might have continued for longer had Queen Victoria been instead King Victor – in other words, a man. But, as a woman, Victoria was barred from succeeding to the throne of Hanover. Nonetheless, although the formal link between the United Kingdom and Hanover snapped with her accession to the throne in 1837, Victoria's own sense of identity was decidedly mixed. In one of her frequent spats with her eldest son, the future Edward VII, she reminded him sharply that his was a German family. She was right. Victoria's forebears were overwhelmingly German. She was married to a German prince, her first cousin, Albert of Saxe-Coburg, and the couple often conversed privately in German.

MADE IN GERMANY

A GOOD RIDDANCE.

[The KING has done a popular act in abolishing the German titles held by members of His Majesty's family.]

Leonard Raven Hill, 'A Good Riddance', *Punch*, 27 June 1917: George V is shown getting rid of the British monarchy's German titles – but only in the third year of the First World War.

The strong German imprint on the modern British monarchy is exemplified by the sumptuous piece of music that has been played at every coronation since 1727: the anthem, 'Zadok the Priest'. Based on texts from the King James Bible, this was composed by the German-born George Frideric Handel, originally for the coronation of George II, who was himself born and brought up in Hanover.

Handel's reference to Zadok, who features in the Old Testament as the priest who anoints King Solomon, points to an important reason why – despite its discontinuous and emphatically transnational history – the monarchy has been able to function as a focus of British union. Virtually all monarchies in history everywhere have possessed and exploited religious associations, and this has emphatically been the case here. The sovereign is Supreme Governor of the Church of England and, from the late seventeenth century, the monarchy was widely viewed as a guarantor and symbol of the predominant Protestantism of Great Britain as a whole, and of the Protestant supremacy in Ireland. It was because the House of Hanover was a Protestant dynasty that most Britons – though not all – were prepared to accept its import and accession to the British throne in 1714. Moreover, as Britain subsequently increased in power and wealth, it became more common for men and women to view it as a new Israel, a chosen nation. It is this seductive idea, and not just the splendid music, which accounts for the invariable inclusion of 'Zadok the Priest' in British coronations. Handel's anthem represents the British monarch as the Lord's anointed. It also conveys the subliminal message that the land over which he or she reigns is indeed Godland.

Over the course of the nineteenth and twentieth centuries, the idea that the monarchy was integral to Britain's providential destiny and prosperity ceased to be identified so powerfully with Protestants, and was strengthened by the course of events. In harsh reality, the British monarchy has been the beneficiary of successive global crises that were almost entirely outside its control. Had the United Kingdom been defeated and/or invaded during the Napoleonic Wars before 1815, or had it been overwhelmed in the First World War or the Second, then monarchy here – as in many other parts of Europe – might well have collapsed or been irredeemably tarnished. As it was, victory in all three of these massive conflicts helped to secure the monarchy's existence, and bestowed on it a kind of superstitious attraction and charisma.

The Crown became for many Britons a sort of lucky charm and emblem, both a force protecting the UK from the calamities that seemed to be overwhelming other European polities, and a marker of this privileged British immunity and well-being. A song composed in Dundee, at a time when Napoleon's armies were still rampaging through much of Continental Europe, celebrated Britain's then reigning monarch, George III, thus:

> For under him we sit and crack,
> In peace and unity compact,
> Whilst every nation's on the rack
> That does nae like our Geordie.

At the time this was composed, George III was actually

blind, senile, and kept largely in seclusion. But the evidence suggests that many of his subjects were still prepared to view him as a totem and protective talisman, the king's very advanced age and evident frailty allowing him to appear a benign, even sacred counterweight to Napoleon Bonaparte. In rather the same way during the 1930s and 40s, first George V and then George VI were widely perceived – and widely represented in the British media – as homely but wholesome alternatives to the dictatorial rulers afflicting parts of Continental Europe: Hitler, Franco and Mussolini.

British monarchs reigning for especially long periods have contributed to political stability, and shaped opinion in another respect. They have helped to conceal from their nominal subjects the full, disturbing extent of change, or at least helped them to sustain it. Thus the sheer length of Queen Victoria's reign – from 1837 to 1901 – almost certainly made it easier for some British and even Irish men and women to come to terms with what was then an unparalleled rate of urban, demographic and technological change. Elizabeth II's reign, which commenced in 1952, is almost as long as Victoria's, and she too has served to conceal change by way of her own apparent changelessness. Never in history has a polity given up ruling as many diverse parts of the globe as rapidly as the United Kingdom has been obliged to do since 1952. Some of its inhabitants, however, may have found this brutal descent from global power easier to bear – and even possible to ignore – because of the present Queen's reassuringly durable reign.

There may be further changes in the future for the

monarchy to strive to gloss over. As we have seen, in the past, individual monarchs often ruled over different and distinct kingdoms, and helped to forge connections between them. We may be on the verge of a revival of this system. The First Minister of Scotland, Alex Salmond, has said that if Scottish voters opt for independence in the 2014 referendum, he wants the House of Windsor to act as monarchs of Scotland. This would be in tandem with, but distinct from, their role as head of state of the rest of the United Kingdom.

If, in the future, a member of the House of Windsor does serve as the sovereign of an independent Scotland – while also maintaining his or her state in England, Wales and Northern Ireland – this will merely underline monarchy's capacity to cover over sharp political change and to create a semblance of continuity where little really exists.

# Part II

# DIVISIONS

# ❻

# ENGLAND

There was once a major panic about the health and future of Englishness. Some commentators argued it was Continental Europeans who were the problem, especially the French. Others blamed Scotland. Scots, they claimed, absorbed a disproportionate amount of Britain's tax revenue, while taking too many of its influential jobs, including that of prime minister. 'Into our places, states and beds they creep,' wrote a particularly angry English poet of Scottish pretensions, 'They've sense to get, what we want sense to keep.' It was vital, many journalists and polemicists argued, to insist on the centrality of England, and to cultivate 'the English name'. 'I beg pardon for the use of so unfashionable a word,' wrote one activist, 'but I must say that I am now an Englishman. I now prefer that word to Briton.'

The language and style of these outbursts give the game away. These are not interventions in current debates about politics and identity (though in essence they easily could be) but comments dating from the 1760s. Across that decade, some Englishmen and women seem to have experienced high levels of anxiety and disorientation, which were sharpened by events on the Continent, and by the appointment of the first ever Scottish prime minister, John Stuart, 3rd earl of Bute.

Anxieties about Englishness have surfaced at other periods of time. During the late nineteenth and early twentieth centuries, growing rivalry with Germany and the United States, and demands for home rule in Ireland, Scotland and Wales, again provoked panic about the security of Englishness. A book from this period, pointedly entitled *The Oppressed English*, took note of the number of 'Celtic' careerists in high civilian and military offices, and the tendency nonetheless to put the blame for all of the faults of Britain and its empire only on the English, while many proposals were advanced both before and after the First World War for England to have its own parliament. 'If home rule for England presents serious problems', argued one journalist in 1911, 'we had better face them at once. They are not going to be solved either by postponing them or ignoring them.'

We seem to be living through another such period of panic and complaint now. Recent surveys suggest that sizeable numbers in England feel they are getting a raw deal from both the European Union and the British Union. Sixty per cent of English people – according to one poll – now believe that Scots get more than their fair share of state funding, while roughly the same percentage feel that London devotes insufficient attention to England's particular needs. And enthusiasm for Englishness is on the rise.

Witness the growing popularity in recent years of celebrating St George's Day.

But *why* exactly have the English been susceptible to periodic bouts of self-scrutiny and anxiety over identity?

After all, in terms of geographical size and wealth, England has always been the preponderant country in these islands. In population terms, too, it has been the biggest player, and is becoming more so. In 1801, 54 per cent of the UK's population lived in England. By 1871, this had risen to almost 70 per cent. Now, England contains over 53 million people, more than five times the total number of inhabitants in Scotland, Wales and Northern Ireland combined. This growing demographic disparity is one reason why support for Welsh and Scottish devolution or independence has increased. As the one-time Canadian prime minister Pierre Trudeau remarked of his country's relationship with the United States, it is not comfortable being a mouse lying next to an elephant: 'No matter how friendly or even-tempered is the beast ... one is affected by every twitch and grunt.' For many in Wales and Scotland, the elephant lying next to them is England, and it is getting more alarming all the time.

There is another respect in which England has been substantially – though not unambiguously – advantaged. It developed a strong, centralised state earlier than its adjacent neighbours, and earlier too than its main Continental competitors.

When William of Normandy invaded England in 1066, he acquired a country already ruled by a single monarchy. Over the next three centuries, law and administration became more standardised, and Parliament established itself as a consistent part of English government. Then there was religion. English monarchs did not assume the title of Supreme Governor of the Church till the Reformation. But even before that, the idea was being fostered that England was God's chosen land; or, as one Bishop put it: 'God is English'. So, if state-making is crucially to do with 'rule by one man at the head of an army, buttressed by as much support from religion as can be mustered', then it is fair to say that England's official classes achieved this with stunning precocity.

England's experience was also precocious in terms of language. Whereas it is estimated that at least a quarter of France's inhabitants still could not speak French as late as the 1860s, English was already the dominant language in England centuries before this, both in official life and in popular usage. The degree to which the English were able, from very early on, to assume the pre-eminence in their country of a single language is shown by the career of Dorothy Pentreath.

Dolly, as she was called, was born in 1692 to a poor fisherman's family in Mousehole in Cornwall, and may have been the last person in history to grow up a monoglot speaker of Cornish. Not till she was twenty, she claimed, did she risk uttering some words of English, and it was not a success. 'I don't want to speak English', she is supposed to have exclaimed on her deathbed in 1777 (in Cornish of course). As this probably apocryphal story suggests, Dolly became something of a celebrity in her lifetime; and, as a single mother in need of funds, she milked this as much as

A 1789 etching based on a painting by John Opie of Dorothy Pentreath.

possible, meeting with tourists and antiquarians and posing for portraits. She was able to make a figure in this way because she seemed a rarity, a freak even: born in a country so early unified in linguistic terms, Dolly lacked English as her cradle tongue.

The fact that their country was by many standards remarkably coherent from very early on seems often to have made for English arrogance and chauvinism, at least among the metropolitan, articulate classes whose reactions were reported. A Venetian traveller grumbled in the 1490s that 'the English are great lovers of themselves', and there are umpteen examples of similar comments by foreign visitors. Yet, as we have seen, confidence – often complacency – about England's importance and distinctiveness have been combined with recurrent episodes of noisy anxiety about the security of this country's identity. Why?

One reason may be the very success of English statemaking. It was in part because they developed a powerful state so early that the English were in a position to invade Wales, Scotland and Ireland in the Middle Ages, and in 1603 to tempt a Scottish king, James VI, to move to London, and thereby establish a union of crowns. These violent encounters and unions with the outer regions of these islands enhanced state power, but may also have muddied an English sense of self. The unfortunate English habit that still lingers of using 'England' as a synonym for the entire island of Britain is often interpreted as one more expression of English arrogance. Might it not also testify to a certain lack of clarity about boundaries and identity?

It is arguable, indeed, that in focusing so relentlessly on

state-making, governments in London have sometimes lost sight of the desirability of devoting creative thought to people-making and people-building: and that this has been especially so in the case of England, which was brought under centralised control so early.

Consider, for instance, education. It was not until 1870 that the Westminster Parliament began to make education compulsory for all children: much later than governments in many other European states. As a result, until the late nineteenth century, there was no guarantee that children in England or Wales (Scotland, with its network of parish schools, seems to have fared better) would receive any instruction about national history, or geography, or citizenship. Even after 1870, the content of history teaching in schools remained random.

To be sure, over the centuries, British governments did sometimes intervene to push the English language in outlying regions where it was weak: in North Wales, the Scottish Highlands, and the south of Ireland. But England's own precocious linguistic uniformity made it seem less problematic as far as effective state intervention was concerned. English cohesion and good order appeared more solid, and perhaps still does. It is striking that, in the 1990s, Wales and Northern Ireland were each accorded devolved national assemblies, and Scotland received its own Edinburgh parliament. England, however, was left to muddle along as before: not so much Cinderella, as the big sister whose reliability could be taken for granted.

Yet it is inappropriate to treat England's unity too much as a given. Like all countries, it contains marked regional variations. It also contains a major and longstanding fault-line.

The American essayist and poet Ralph Waldo Emerson took note of this when he toured England in the mid nineteenth century. 'What we think of when we talk of English traits', he wrote, 'really narrows itself to a small district ... 'tis a very restricted nationality. As you go north ... the world's Englishman is no longer found.' What Emerson meant by this was that England is bottom-heavy. In wealth, status, power, population, and in key cultural terms, it is weighted heavily towards the South. The prime archbishopric of the Church of England is in Canterbury in Kent. Traditionally, the most prestigious English universities have been Oxford and Cambridge. British army officers are trained at Sandhurst in Surrey, while their naval counterparts train at Dartmouth in Devon. Then, of course, there is London, the 'great wen' as William Cobbett called it, a pathological swelling on the face of the nation.

At one level, London's size, wealth, power, cultural energy, multiple roles, glittering prizes and sheer density of population have, over the centuries, made it a highly effective centripetal force both in England and within these islands as a whole. London has also been a remarkable melting pot and a busy arena for multifarious ideas and contacts. In *The Prelude* William Wordsworth wrote of the swirling multiplicity of London's streets:

> Thou endless stream of men and moving
>    things ...
> The Jew; the stately and slow-moving Turk,

With freight of slippers piled beneath his arm ...
Among the crowd all specimens of man,
Through all the colours which the sun bestows,
And every character of form and face;
The Swede, the Russian; from the genial south,
The Frenchman and the Spaniard; from remote
America, the Hunter-Indian; Moors,
Malays, Lascars, the Tartar, the Chinese,
And Negro Ladies in white muslin gowns.

When Wordsworth wrote these lines about London, the metropolis was already a world city, in fact *the* world city, with the biggest urban population on the globe. London has long since lost that status, but it remains indisputably a world city. Producing almost 22 per cent of the UK's total output, and with a population bigger than Wales and Scotland combined, London could easily become a city-state on its own, and a very rich one. As we will see, London's disproportionate power has been an acute challenge to the English North. It is also something of a challenge to English identity more broadly. No countries are homogeneous, and nor should they strive to be. But in regard to the challenges posed by its unique, over-mighty metropolis, as in many other respects, England arguably suffers from the lack of a discrete forum in which its particular internal disparities and inequities might be analysed and addressed.

L. S. Lowry, *Coming from the Mill*, pastel, *c.* 1917–18

# 7

# NORTH AND SOUTH

In the summer of 2013 Tate Britain staged a major exhibition of the work of L. S. Lowry, the first in a great London gallery since 1976, when the artist died. Most of this recent exhibition, *Lowry and the Painting of Modern Life*, was given over to his paintings of Manchester, the city where he grew up, and of one of its metropolitan boroughs, Salford, where Lowry kept himself going by working part-time as a rent-collector. These townscapes have become famous and are immensely popular, with their rows of square mills and red terraced houses grimed with soot, their factory chimneys protruding into white-grey skies, their dour chapels and slag heaps, their cynically polluted waterways, and their swarming skeletal inhabitants, who appear oddly isolated figures even when Lowry shows them scurrying to a football match or gathering at a fair.

Lowry's paintings have deeply influenced how we imagine not just industrial life, but also the English North. In some respects, his canvases have been too influential, not least because the North, of course, is actually very large and scenically variegated. A recent study by researchers at the University of Sheffield suggests that in order to visualise and understand the North–South divide we need to think of an imaginary line running from where the River Severn meets the sea on the western side of England, across to the Wash on the coastline of eastern England. Although this notional line sometimes dips into the old counties of Gloucestershire, Warwickshire, Leicestershire and Lincolnshire, the bulk of these counties and all the areas of England below them, make up the South. Above this notional line there is the North. And as far as life chances are concerned (and much else), conditions become very different, very rapidly once you cross the line.

To be sure, there are pockets of deep, complacent prosperity in the English North (think of Knutsford or Tatton in Cheshire) just as there are areas of sharp poverty in the South (think of Dagenham or Peckham in London). Nonetheless, if you live north of the line, whether in England or Scotland, you are on average more likely to die before the age of seventy-five than people in the South, while if you are a teenager living south of the line you are on average more likely to win admission to an elite Russell Group University than are your English counterparts in the North.

Disparities between the North and the South in terms of wealth and living standards seem to go back at least to medieval times. A tendency to caricature and 'other' the North also goes back centuries. Last year, a peer caused uproar in the House of Lords when he suggested that fracking – forcing open rocks so as to extract oil and gas – should be avoided in 'sensitive' environments such as Sussex, but implemented instead in 'uninhabited and desolate areas' like the English north-east. There are ample precedents for this kind of metropolitan mental distancing. Told that his army regiment was transferring from Brighton on the south coast to Manchester, the London-born Regency dandy known as Beau Brummell protested only half-jokingly that he had not reckoned on having to serve abroad.

As the American Civil War reminds us, North–South divides have characterised many different polities, and they exist in Wales, Scotland and (manifestly) the island of Ireland, not just England. Yet the sharpest of these North–South divisions as far as Great Britain is concerned – that within England – has been less scrutinised than the differences between the English, Scots, and Welsh. In part, I suspect, this is because politicians and nationalists, and even historians, prefer to think in terms of entire countries than pay close attention to complicating and troublesome subdivisions. Margaret Thatcher, who sometimes styled herself an 'English nationalist' and spent most of her career in London, dismissed the North–South divide as a myth. But the divide is real and important, though *the ways* in which it has been important have changed markedly over time.

Before the early seventeenth century, conditions in the English North were shaped not just by its distance from London, but also by its proximity to, and partial involvement in, the independent kingdom of Scotland. Until the thirteenth century, Scottish kings periodically controlled large parts of Northumbria and southern Cumbria; while Berwick on Tweed changed hands violently at least a dozen times before finally coming under English control in 1482.

The fact that sections of the North formed a contested border zone in this way at least meant that London had to pay persistent attention to it. During the thirteenth and fourteenth centuries, Edward I, Edward II and Edward III all used York, then the premier northern city, as a capital for parts of their reigns. And, from the fifteenth century to the 1640s, a Council of the North was in operation, with special jurisdiction for most of England north of the Humber.

But as Anglo-Scottish relations gradually eased in the seventeenth century, and the North came to seem more secure, London's interest in it waned. Like Wales, Ireland and Scotland, the English North has often been placed at a disadvantage by the disproportionate concentration of wealth, power, status and population in and around the capital in the South. To a much greater extent than was the case in Scotland, the North of England also long suffered from an educational deficit.

It possessed outstanding grammar and charity schools. But there were no universities in the North of England until 1832, and while Durham University was established that year, this remained the only northern English university until 1880. Ambitious northerners in search of higher education either had to go abroad, or to a Scottish university, or migrate south, which many of them did. Some of the cultural repercussions of this still persist. Here is an example. Because advanced education in England was concentrated for so long in the South, in what is still indicatively called the 'golden triangle', Oxford, Cambridge, and ultimately London, it was this region that tended to set the standard for the 'correct' use of the English language. It was largely southern-talk and southern usage that came to be regarded as 'the King's English', a phrase that was popularised in a 1906 book by two Kentish-born, Oxbridge-educated brothers, Henry Watson Fowler and George Fowler. Other English regions' modes of speaking were often treated as mere dialects, and sometimes dismissed as socially incorrect and disreputable.

For a time, however, the deepening influence of the Industrial Revolution modified the balance of power. The North was able to capitalise on rich reserves of coal, iron and water, and its industrial cities mushroomed, sucking in migrants not just from surrounding rural areas, but also from Scotland, Wales, Ireland, and even the English South and other parts of Europe. In 1800, Bradford in West Yorkshire had only a couple of thousand residents. By 1911, it was a city of 300,000 souls, while its Lancashire neighbour, Manchester, had exploded into the ninth biggest city in the world.

We can see some of the downsides of this sort of rapid industrial and urban expansion in parts of India and China today: child labour, terrible industrial accidents, epidemic disease, overcrowded slums, poor sanitation, vicious exploitation, environmental pollution. In Britain, the violence that pioneering industrialisation sometimes inflicted on the environment and human beings only deepened at one level the consciousness that the North was different. Elizabeth Gaskell's significantly titled novel *North and South*, published in 1855, is set in a smoke-filled northern town called Milton, which is based on Manchester, and describes the shock experienced by an incoming young woman, Margaret Hale, who has grown up in a gentle southern village, but who now witnesses the precarious

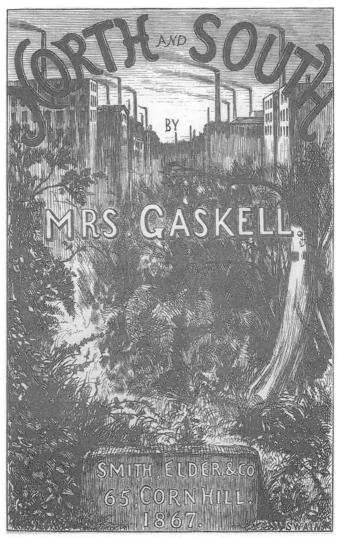

An illustration by George du Maurier for an 1867
edition of Elizabeth Gaskell's *North and South*.

lives of the town's workers, and the brutality of some of its employers.

Gaskell was perceptive enough to recognise, however, that there was more to the industrial North than urban squalor, mass alienation, and smoke-filled air that required lace curtains to be laundered every week. Not only was industrialisation generating new wealth and new sorts of prosperous people, it was also helping to engineer modernity. At one point in *North and South*, Gaskell evokes the force of men and machines in a Milton foundry: 'the men like demons in their fire and soot colouring ... awaiting the moment when the tons of solid iron should have melted down into fiery liquid'. What she is conveying is at once a new kind of industrial hell, and simultaneously new forms of power and creativity and human confidence.

This new confidence and power – a sense that parts of the North at least could now claim parity with the South in terms of national (and global) significance and the generation of wealth and culture – is reflected in many of the most splendid Victorian civic buildings: St George's Hall in Liverpool, for instance, with its lavish floors of Minton tiles, and its interior columns commemorating art, science, fortitude and justice, and the town halls constructed slightly later at Leeds, Halifax, Manchester, Sheffield and Bradford. A conviction that they were building a new world, helping to construct modernity, was also shared by some of those working in northern cities, including men and women employed on the factory floor. J. B. Priestley recalled a visit to Yorkshire in the early 1930s:

One unmarried elderly woman of my acquaintance, up there had just retired, after working fifty years as a weaver in one mill. During that time, she and her relatives and most of her friends had not only worked in that enormous mill but had lived all their lives in its shadow ... Fifty years, only broken by an occasional four or five days at Morecambe or Blackpool. Fifty years, living in the same back-to-back houses, just behind the mill. Millions of yards of fine fabrics had gone streaming out, from their hands, to almost every part of the world ... Fifty years of quick skilled work, with hours, in winter, lasting from dark to dark. If a world that once went bare is now partly clothed and decorated with fabrics, then these folk may be said to have lent a hand in the great processes of civilization; they have not been passengers in the ship.

Priestley came from a suburb of Bradford, where his headmaster father is supposed to have refused to read London-produced newspapers on the grounds that he had no interest in events down South. Partly because of cultural snobbery, Priestley himself is still sometimes dismissed as a soft-focused, nostalgic, overly middlebrow writer. Yet he was appalled by what the slump and depression of the 1920s and 30s did to his home district and other industrial regions – 'the producing England' of the North – and sharply and radically angry at the equanimity with which many London financiers seemed to be regarding manufacturing blight: 'What had the City done for its old ally, the industrial North?' he wrote in *English Journey* (1934): 'It seemed to have done what the black-moustached glossy gentleman in the old melodramas always did to the innocent maiden.'

It was not so much industrial capitalism, however, but the neglect and decline of industry at which Priestley raged. Consequently, unlike Lowry, the part-time rent-collector and paternalist Tory who hardly ever chose to paint men and women actively at work, Priestley was aware – and prepared to argue – that even exploited factory hands might find some satisfaction in making things, in feeling that they were more than just 'passengers in the ship'.

And for as long as northern England continued as a major centre of industry and manufacturing – and was still perceived as such – the divide between it and the English South remained controlled. Electoral politics help to illustrate this. In the 1945 general election, which they lost badly, half of the Conservative Party's ten safest seats were nonetheless still located in northern England. The same was true in the 1951 election, which the Conservatives won. In other words, in the mid twentieth century, the North was genuinely in balance between the two main political parties. As the terminal decline of heavy industry became increasingly apparent, this changed. Now, and as far as electoral results are concerned, most of the South of England outside central London is deep blue. By contrast, and as a journalist reported last year, 'save for a belt of Tory hills and dales across North Yorkshire and the Lake District, the North is red'. Although much has been said and written recently about a revival of Englishness, there seems again to be at least two rather different Englands in play, North and South.

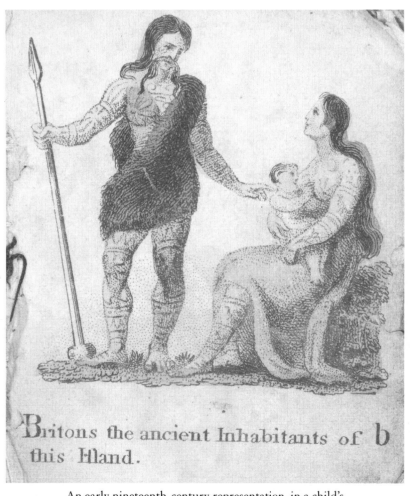

Britons the ancient Inhabitants of b
this Island.

An early nineteenth-century representation, in a child's
alphabet book, of Welsh 'Ancient Britons'.

# 8

# WALES

Towards the end of *A Man for all Seasons*, the 1966 film of Robert Bolt's play about Sir Thomas More, there is a telling episode to do with Wales. On trial for high treason for resisting Henry VIII's marital and religious projects, More is finally doomed to the scaffold by the perjury of one Richard Rich. A singularly ruthless Tudor politician in real life as in the play, Rich, we learn, has been bribed into giving false testimony by being appointed Attorney General for Wales. More turns on him with a gentle but devastating rebuke: 'For Wales? Why, Richard, it profits a man nothing to give his soul for the whole world – but for Wales?'

There are several reasons why these lines – which Bolt invented – invariably provoke laughter, and one of them is an element of prejudice.* Wales is a small country. It contains about 5 per cent of the United Kingdom's population; and, at some 8000 square miles, it is less than a sixth of the size of England, and roughly only a quarter of the size of

* It may be relevant that Bolt (1924–95) was born in Sale, Cheshire, a county with a historically close but uneven relationship with North Wales.

Scotland or the island of Ireland. Moreover, unlike Ireland, Scotland and England, Wales has never been treated as a kingdom, only a principality. Consequently – and again unlike Ireland, Scotland and England – Wales has never been emblematically represented on the Union Jack. A component part of this polity, it is missing from its flag. Wales – *or so it can appear* – succumbed to London's control earlier and more thoroughly than either Scotland or Ireland, while also being less inclined to struggle. 'The outstanding fact about Wales', wrote a Welsh nationalist bitterly in 1942, '... is that she has always been a nation on the defensive.'

Yet responses in Wales to attempted acts of union have been both stubborn and creative, and are revealing about more than itself.

Paradoxically, a good starting-point from which to begin examining why, is the remarkable chain of castles built by Edward I at Flint, Beaumaris, Conwy, Harlech, Caernarfon and elsewhere, after his conquest and annexation of Wales in the late thirteenth century. At one level, these colossal fortresses are plainly monuments to colonisation: 'magnificent badges of our subjection', in the words of an eighteenth-century Welsh antiquarian. Caernarfon Castle, for instance, was designed to echo the walls of Constantinople and imperial Rome, and was begun in 1283, a year after the killing of the last indigenous Prince of Wales, Llywelyn ap Gruffydd. It was supposedly in Caernarfon Castle's 'Eagle Tower', ornamented with stone imperial eagles, that Edward I's own son was born: and so began the tradition of English and subsequently British monarchs, appropriating the title 'Prince of Wales' for their own first male offspring.

The other side of this English aggression, however, was its enormous effort and expense. Edward I's Welsh conquests are estimated to have cost him at least ten times his regular annual income as king, which indicates how vital an acquisition Wales was deemed to be, while Edward's elaborate system of castles also demonstrates how much, and with good cause, he feared that the Welsh might continue to resist and rebel.

Wales still appeared only partly under control in the 1530s, which is why Thomas Cromwell – Sir Thomas More's nemesis – provided for what, long after, came to be styled 'Acts of Union'. By an act of 1536, supplemented in 1543, Wales was declared 'for ever from henceforth incorporated, united, and annexed to and with this ... realm of England'. English systems of law and administration were imposed on the country. It was divided into shires, supplied with a system of JPs, and given MPs at Westminster. It was also stipulated that English should be the language of Welsh law courts, and that monoglot Welsh speakers were ineligible for public office. Willingness to learn English was to be the key to attaining any official status in Wales.

Some three hundred years later, in 1835, the historian and Whig politician Thomas Babington Macaulay famously argued that English, 'the language spoken by the ruling class', should be the only medium of subsidised education in British India, so as to 'form a class who may be interpreters between us and the millions whom we govern; a class of persons, Indian in blood and colour, but English in taste, in opinions, in morals, and in intellect'. This was essentially what the legislation of 1536 and 1543 was designed to encourage in regard to Wales, and essentially what for centuries was achieved: an effective, on-side Welsh ruling class that was fluent in English, and that behaved in a similar (though not identical) fashion to its counterparts in England.

As this suggests, there were some marked parallels between how London sought at different times to implement control over the outer zones of the British Isles, and some of the methods of rule, organisation and influence it later tried to deploy in Britain's overseas empire. Yet it is important to recognise that the Welsh, too, nurtured imperial projects and imperial myths.

Until the twelfth century, much of what is now Wales was commonly referred to in Latin writings as 'Britannia', while Welsh people seem regularly to have referred to themselves as 'Britons'. These facts were drawn on and embroidered by Geoffrey of Monmouth in his widely influential and popular histories. In the *History of the Kings of Britain*, produced in the late 1130s, and in two equally inventive works on Merlin, he claimed that legendary Welsh princes, including Uther Pendragon and King Arthur, had once ruled over the entirety of Britain, and that the prophecies of Merlin suggested that, one day, the Welsh would 'win back … the land all together … They will call it Britain again'. These notions acquired fresh currency when the Tudor/Tewdwr dynasty, which was partly Welsh, seized the English throne in 1485. Henry Tudor defeated Richard III at Bosworth that year under a standard that flaunted the red dragon of Wales, and with an army a third of which was Welsh.

John Dee, the remarkable Welsh polymath who worked in London and who was sometimes consulted by Queen Elizabeth I, also propagated ideas about the quintessential

Welshness of Britain. It may have been Dee who invented the phrase 'British Empire'. Certainly he claimed that a Welsh prince named Madoc had succeeded in 'discovering' America some 300 years before Christopher Columbus. Consequently, Dee argued, Elizabeth I possessed an undoubted right to colonise in America. But this right, he insisted, rested on what initially had been Welsh exploits and Welsh initiatives.

These ideas circulated widely in print and manuscript until at least the eighteenth century, and the notion that Britain – and its empire – had originally been *Welsh* creations seems to have allowed some men and women in Wales to rationalise and cope with the loss of their country's independence. These same ideas and myths also made it easier for some of them to develop dual identities: to view themselves as Welsh, yes, but also as British.

The sense of Wales's distinctiveness, however, persisted. It was sustained not just by the country's landscape, folk customs and music, modes of dress and cuisine and Protestant belief, but crucially by language. Although London insisted on the use of English in law and administration in Wales, it also wanted to propagate and entrench the Protestant Reformation. This ensured parliamentary support for proposals that the Bible and Book of Common Prayer should be translated into Welsh and widely distributed. The most notable result of these policies was the publication in 1588 of William Morgan's magnificent translation of the Bible, as important a text in Wales as the King James Bible has been in Scotland and England. Here, for instance, is Morgan's wonderful rendition of the 23rd Psalm, 'The Lord is my Shepherd':

*Psalm 23: Beibl 1588*

Yr Arglwydd yw fy mugail: ni bydd eisiau arnaf.

Efe a bâr im orwedd mewn porfeydd gwelltog;
    efe a'm tywys gerllaw dyfroedd tawel.

Efe a ddychwel fy enaid, ac a'm harwain ar hyd
    llwybrau cyfiawnder er mwyn ei enw.

A phe rhodiwn ar hyd glyn cysgod angau nid
    ofnaf niwed, oherwydd dy fod ti gyda mi: dy
    wialen a'th ffon a'm cysurant.

Ti a arlwyi ford ger fy mron yn erbyn fy ngwrthwynebwyr:
    iraist fy mhen ag olew, fy ffiol sydd lawn.

Daioni a thrugaredd yn ddiau a'm canlynant oll
    ddyddiau fy mywyd, a phreswyliaf yn nhŷ'r
    Arglwydd yn dragywydd.

The constant repetition of such majestic prose in churches and chapels in Wales, and its availability for private reading at home, helped to ensure that Welsh survived and evolved as a written language as well as a mode of speech. Until the second half of the nineteenth century, most people in Wales seem to have dealt overwhelmingly in their own language. When an English clergyman named Thomas Bowles was appointed to a parish in Anglesey in 1766, he found only one family there, plus one other person, able (and willing) to converse with him in his own cradle tongue – this out of a community of 500 people. The number of Welsh speakers, as a proportion of the total Welsh population, only began seriously to decline in the late Victorian era.

By then, Wales had become a very different country, and both more and less distinctive. In Wales, as in the north

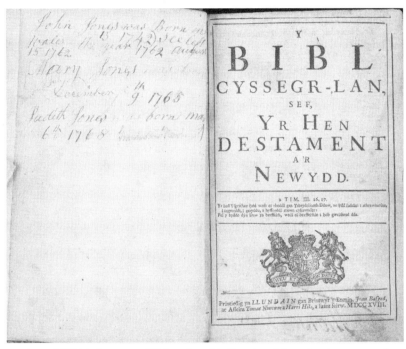

A 1718 Welsh-language Bible printed in London. Note the signatures of successive Welsh owners, and the prominence given to the royal coat of arms.

of England, industrialisation damaged the landscape and devastated the lives of many human beings. But it also led to a rise in wealth and population, and it altered somewhat the balance of power within the island of Great Britain.

By the late nineteenth century, the Royal Navy was fuelled by Welsh coal, and South Wales had become the biggest coal producer in the world. By 1820, the Swansea area was already producing 90 per cent of the UK's copper, while children in schools throughout these islands were writing on tablets made out of slate mined and quarried in North Wales, at Penrhyn, Dinorwig and Blaenau Ffestiniog. As had been the case in the English North, the explosion of new industrial opportunities in Wales sucked in migrants from elsewhere. Between 1780 and 1860, the Welsh population more than doubled, and urbanisation grew. More shops were established in Merthyr Tydfil between 1830 and 1850, than in any other town in Britain, while Cardiff's population expanded eighty-fold between 1801 and 1901 – one reason why in 1905 it was formally recognised as a city.

The impact of these changes on Welsh identity was mixed. Especially in South Wales, inward migration seems to have weakened the grip of the Welsh language. Welsh industrialisation also drew in large amounts of English capital, thereby creating new channels for influence from without. But there were also gains. Wales's expanding railways, another outcrop of industrialisation, brought its northern and southern regions into far greater contact than before, making possible a more unified Welsh national identity. As had been the case in the north of England, new industrial wealth also provided Wales with greater leverage within the United Kingdom, an enhanced sense of its own importance, and increased sources of local cultural sponsorship and patronage. By the outbreak of the First World War, Wales possessed its own university system, its own National Library and Museum, its own recognised national anthem, 'Hen Wlad Fy Nhadau'/'Land of my Fathers', and – in the brilliant and charismatic David Lloyd George – a future British prime minister.

Wales had also come closer to a measure of self-government. It is sometimes supposed that the devolution measures of the 1990s represented a novel departure in political thinking and experimentation in the United Kingdom, but this is hardly the case. Welsh self-government was openly canvassed by politicians in the late nineteenth century, and not least by Lloyd George. The prospect divided Welsh opinion, but it won some powerful converts in Parliament. In 1895 there was a motion in the House of Commons 'to devolve upon Legislatures in Ireland, Scotland, Wales *and* England ... the management and control of their domestic affairs'. In 1911, Winston Churchill called for separate parliaments for Wales, Scotland and Ireland, and for regional assemblies in England. Two years later, there was a major debate in the Lords on whether the UK should become a federal state, with separate parliaments in each of its component parts.

We can therefore view devolution, which in Wales has given rise to a National Assembly in Cardiff, as in part a resumption of interrupted business. It marks a return to trends and ideas which were already in evidence before 1914, but which were then largely put on hold by the need to fight two unprecedented world wars.

A railway poster designed by Frank H. Mason, *c.* 1932, evokes – for an American audience – the scenic distinctiveness of parts of Scotland.

# SCOTLAND

On 10 August 1987, Liz Lochhead's *Mary Queen of Scots Got Her Head Chopped Off* premiered at the Edinburgh Festival. Ostensibly, the play focuses on the relationship between Mary Stuart, who succeeded to the throne of Scotland in 1542, just six days old, and her cousin, Elizabeth I of England:

> Once upon a time there were twa queens on the wan green island, and the wan green island was split intae twa kingdoms. But no *equal* kingdoms, naebody in their richt mind would insist on that.
>
> For the northern kingdom was cauld and sma. And the people were low-statured and ignorant and feart o their lords and poor … The other kingdom in the island was large, and prosperous, with wheat and barley and fat kye in the fields o' her yeoman fermers, and wool in her looms, and beer in her barrels and, at the mouth of her greatest river, a great port, a glistening city that sucked

all wealth to its centre – which was a palace and a court of a queen. She was a cousin, a clever cousin, a wee bit aulder, and mibbe no sae braw as the other queen, but a queen nevertheless.

Queen o a country wi' an army, an a navy and dominion over many lands.

Twa queens. Wan green island.

As this wonderful opening evocation suggests, Lochhead – who is now the Scots *Makar* or national poet – used the rivalry between Mary and Elizabeth to comment more broadly on the state of affairs between Scotland and England. As she admits, her take on the Virgin Queen was coloured by her reactions to Margaret Thatcher, not a popular figure north of the border by the late 1980s. Lochhead's stage directions have Elizabeth I speaking in clipped, old-fashioned tones and also sometimes assuming masculine costume. By contrast, Mary in the play speaks broad Scots with a French accent ('not English', Lochhead stipulated) and is conspicuously female. In this vision of Mary and Elizabeth – as in some of the ongoing debates on the referendum on Scottish independence – Scotland and England are represented as emphatically different.

Yet the real Mary Queen of Scots and Elizabeth I actually possessed much in common. They were both female sovereigns challenged by having to operate in a man's world. They were both highly intelligent, cultured and physically charismatic Renaissance princesses; and their fates and political projects were inextricably linked. The Catholic Mary arguably plotted against the Protestant

86

Elizabeth, but she also cherished her own claim to the English throne. Elizabeth I held Mary in confinement and finally ordered her execution. But she also named Mary's son as her own successor. To this extent, these long-dead female rulers do indeed throw light on wider Anglo-Scottish relations. They stand as a reminder that Scotland and England have been characterised by similarities as well as differences, and that these two countries have been persistently but diversely interconnected.

The connections in question have sometimes been violent. Between 1040 and the Battle of Culloden in 1746, it has been calculated, every monarch in London except three either had to repel a Scottish invasion of England, or chose to invade Scotland, or in some cases did both these things. These recurrent military conflicts underline the point that, whereas London was able to bring Wales under some level of control relatively early, Scotland proved far more intractable. English armies never succeeded in conquering the country in its entirety for any extended period of time. Indeed, for all the disparities in size and wealth between Scotland and England, the border sometimes shifted to the advantage of the former. In the early twelfth century, Scottish kings briefly established dominion over north Lancashire and parts of Yorkshire, as well as over all of Cumberland and Northumberland.

The border between England and Scotland was porous in more than just military terms. Although one in five Scots may still have spoken Gaelic even in the mid eighteenth century, by 1500 English was already the dominant language in the Scottish Lowlands. So people on both sides of the border were able to communicate with each other, cut deals, migrate, intermarry, and exchange ideas. These cross-border exchanges became even more important with the Protestant Reformation, a point made again by the careers of Mary Queen of Scots and Elizabeth I. Mary was deposed in 1567 by some of her own Protestant nobility, and many of these Scottish lords, along with the leader of the Scottish Reformation, John Knox, were in communication with London and the court of Elizabeth I. Conversely, some English Catholics backed Mary's claim to the throne of England, which was why in the end Elizabeth destroyed her.

After the Reformation, the question of *whether* there should be a union between Scotland and England, now both Protestant powers, gradually gave way to arguments over *what type* of union this might be. When Mary's son, James VI of Scotland, also succeeded to the English throne in 1603, he sought to style himself 'King of Great Britain', claimed descent from King Arthur and therefore Welsh antecedents, and attempted unsuccessfully to create a union of parliaments. James was an ardent proponent of a kind of British Protestant imperium. He dispatched Scottish and English settlers to Catholic Ireland, clamped down on the autonomy of the Orkney and Shetland islands, and – more constructively – provided for one of the most significant Unionist texts, the Authorised Version of the Bible, commissioned by King James in 1604, completed seven years later, and increasingly used in worship on both sides of the border, and in Britain's expanding overseas empire.

It was *in part* a perceived threat to Protestantism – war with Louis XIV of France – that helped to persuade most

Scottish and English politicians finally to agree to a parliamentary union in 1707. But far more than the union with Wales, this union was from the outset a compromise, a stand-off even. Scots lost their ancient parliament at Edinburgh, receiving instead (limited) representation in the Westminster Parliament. The cross of St Andrew, the saltire, was blazoned on flags and banners alongside the cross of St George and, on paper, England, Wales and Scotland were all subsumed into 'one united Kingdom by the name of Great Britain', with a single legislature in London, the same Protestant ruler, similar fiscal arrangements, and one system of free trade.

But Scotland retained its own systems of Roman law and local government, its own parish schools and excellent universities (more extensive in number in 1707 than their English counterparts) and its own forms of Protestantism and Presbyterian church government. Especially during the first half-century following parliamentary Union, Scotland still struck most English visitors as substantially foreign. 'The first town' you came to after crossing the border, wrote the novelist Daniel Defoe, with some exaggeration, was 'as perfectly Scots, as if you were a hundred miles north of Edinburgh; nor is there the least appearance of any thing English ... in their way of living, eating, dress or behaviour.' And just as episodes of anti-Scottish prejudice sometimes erupted in eighteenth-century England, English individuals venturing across the border occasionally encountered mockery or worse. When Defoe toured Ross and Cromarty in the northern Highlands, he found it safer to pass himself off as a Frenchman.

The fact that this was a flexible and in many respects only a partial union helps to explain why it has endured for so long. Much of the time, London practised a kind of indirect rule, relying heavily on one or more major Scottish political actors, who in turn used their power and leverage to extract advantages for fellow Scots. Indicatively, such political managers were often nicknamed kings in tacit recognition of Scotland's continuing quasi-autonomy. In the late eighteenth century, a one-time lawyer turned political operator, Henry Dundas, 1st Viscount Melville, alias Harry the Ninth, filled this role. It was partly due to him that, by 1800, a third of all British state sinecures were held by Scots. An equivalent though far less corrupt figure was Tom Johnston, Labour MP for West Stirlingshire, who was Secretary of State for Scotland during the Second World War. The 'King of Scotland', as Winston Churchill called him, Johnston used his power to secure wartime industries, hydro-electric power, and social programmes for Scotland, even establishing a kind of prototype national health service.

Such glittering careers point to one of the persistent lures of the Union, namely, that it has always offered some highly ambitious Scots a bigger, more lucrative stage on which to make a name. The last three British prime ministers – Tony Blair, Gordon Brown, and now David Cameron – have all been either Scottish-born or come from Scottish families. Yet it would be wrong to place too much emphasis on individual self-interest and on economic profits as cements of the Union. Paradoxical though it may seem, British union appealed to many Scots in the past as

A caricature by Richard Newton in 1796 shows torrents of ambitious Scots descending on jobs in Ireland, the West Indies, North America, Hanover, and especially London, which is signposted 'the best road for a Scot'.

an expression of, and vehicle for Scottishness, even as a form of nationalism.

Consider the massive Scottish input over the centuries into the British Empire. Certainly, this provided multitudes of Scots with money, land, trade, commodities, opportunities and jobs, sometimes very important jobs. Between 1850 and 1939, a third of all British colonial governors were Scots. But participation in the British Empire also attracted and excited because it offered a means by which Scots could spread their distinctive educational, religious, cultural and political ideas and traditions across the globe. The empire was British, yes, but it was also Scottish, in some colonial locations – such as Hong Kong – almost overwhelmingly so.

The degree to which British unionism appeared reconcilable with Scottish national consciousness, even nationalism of a sort, helps to explain why – for a long time – pressure groups for greater Scottish autonomy nonetheless clung fast to some of the language and rituals of Britishness. Thus the National Association for the Vindication of Scottish Rights, founded in 1853 to agitate for increased Scottish representation at Westminster, and for limits on the intrusive power of London, made a point nonetheless of toasting the British monarchy at its meetings. 'The more Union, the better,' one of the members of this association argued, 'provided ... the rights of all parties be respected. Union obviates war, encourages commerce, permits of free transit, abolishes national antipathy. Union – provided it be union and not domination – brings equals together for common benefit.' By the same token, the Scottish Covenant

Movement, which flourished in the 1940s and early 1950s, and organised petitions in support of Scottish self-rule, made clear that it did so 'in all loyalty to the Crown and within the framework of the United Kingdom'.

So what changed? And why has change apparently been so rapid? The Scottish National Party, the SNP, did not succeed in winning a seat at Westminster at a general election until 1970. Now, it is the largest party in Scotland, forms the Scottish government, and has stage-managed the referendum on independence. We have already seen some of the reasons for this revolution, not least the decline of once-powerful constitutive stories of British identity, and the shrinkage of manufacturing industry which damaged opportunities and livelihoods in lowland Scotland as in northern England. But important too has been, not so much *a rise* in Scottish nationalism, as the emergence of a different *kind* of Scottish nationalism.

When visiting Scotland in the past few years I have been struck by how many Scots complain about feeling 'colonised' by the English and/or by London. In historical fact, Scotland has never been a colony. It was never conquered, or forced to submit to waves of alien settlers as Ireland was. But historical facts are not the point here. Nationalist movements always rewrite history. To claim that Scotland is a colony is to assert that it is imprisoned within the United Kingdom. It is a way of arguing that Britishness is no longer a useful vehicle – an older form of Scottish national expression – but rather an encumbrance and an oppression. We will have to see which mode of Scottish self-consciousness triumphs on 18 September.

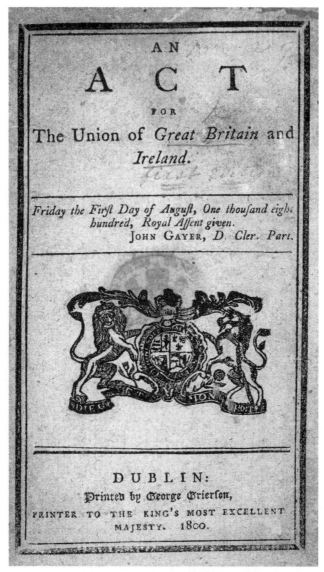

AN

A C T

FOR

The Union of *Great Britain* and *Ireland.*

*Friday the First Day of August, One thousand eight hundred, Royal Assent given.*
JOHN GAYER, D. Cler. Parl.

D U B L I N:

Printed by George Grierson,

PRINTER TO THE KING'S MOST EXCELLENT MAJESTY. 1800.

Title page of An Act for the Union of Great Britain and Ireland, produced in Dublin by the King's Printer, 1800.

# 10

# IRELAND

In 1975 Seamus Heaney published a poem entitled 'Act of Union', of which this is an extract:

> … Your back is a firm line of eastern coast
> And arms and legs are thrown
> Beyond the gradual hills. I caress
> The heaving province where our past has grown.
> I am the tall kingdom over your shoulder
> That you would neither cajole nor ignore.
> Conquest is a lie. I grow older
> Conceding your half-independent shore
> Within whose borders now my legacy
> Culminates inexorably
> And I am still imperially
> Male, leaving you with pain,
> The rending process in the colony,
> The battering ram, the boom burst from within.
> The act sprouted an obstinate fifth column
> Whose stance is growing unilateral …

Heaney sometimes employed metaphors drawn from marriage and sexual intercourse to write about the resolution of opposites, and much of his poetry involves a pressing against boundaries, developing open positions on issues that concern territory, competing histories and identities. But 'Act of Union' is different. Composed in the shadow of the Troubles that erupted in Northern Ireland in the late 1960s, the poem and its politics appear stark. The Act of Union of the title is the one that came into force between Great Britain and Ireland on 1 January 1801, and that persisted for 120 years. In the poem, the Act becomes a rape, perpetrated by an imperially male Britain upon a female Ireland who turns her back in pain and revulsion. As with all rape, this one has enduring consequences. It breeds 'an obstinate fifth column' – in other words, Protestant-dominated Ulster, Northern Ireland – where Heaney was born in 1939 in a Catholic household, and which he left for the Republic of Ireland in 1972, three years before completing 'Act of Union'.

There are those in Great Britain, Northern Ireland, the Irish Republic and elsewhere who still hold to this poem's raw, schematic version of the past. But I want to suggest that what has been involved between varieties of people in the island of Britain and varieties of people in the island of Ireland is not a single act of union so much as several acts, all compromised in different ways.

To be sure, for much of history these two islands have seemed set too close for comfort. Parts of Scotland and the north of Ireland are only twelve miles apart by sea, and Irish peoples are known to have invaded the Scottish

Highlands and Islands from at least the sixth century AD. Anglo-Norman invasions of Ireland began in the twelfth century, with Scottish settlers arriving a century later. But it was the Reformation of the sixteenth century that over-determined relations between the two islands. Protestant-ism succeeded in most of England, Wales and Scotland, but not in Ireland, and this had multiple and protracted consequences. Until the mid nineteenth century, the main military powers in Continental Europe were Catholic. Consequently, for successive governments in London, Ire-land became an all too obvious Achilles heel, a place where a Continental Catholic enemy might invade, rally co-reli-gionist support, and then embark on a further invasion of Britain itself. Both Spain and France sought at regular intervals to do precisely this.

These strategic considerations – and Protestant zeal – were used to legitimise Anglo-Scottish violence against Ireland. In 1541 Henry VIII proclaimed himself king of Ireland, and from the 1570s the formerly slow infiltration of English and Scottish settlers into Ireland gathered pace, and was backed by military force. In 1641, the year of a major rising, Catholics still retained close to two-thirds of all land in Ireland. By the early eighteenth century, after further bouts of civil war and ruthless plantation making, Protestants – who now formed around a fifth of Ireland's population – held over three-quarters of its land. Penal laws disqualified Catholics from sitting in Ireland's parlia-ment in Dublin, debarred them from its only university, Trinity College Dublin, and – at least on paper – prevented them from purchasing land.

You might think on the basis of all this that the London-made and enforced Act of Union of 1800–1801 was bound to fail. It was passed at a time of worldwide warfare and multiple revolutions and in the aftermath of resurgent violence in Ireland itself, a massive rebellion in 1798 characterised again by sectarian slaughter. The 1790s also witnessed two innovations that would press hard on the future: the creation of the Orange Order, dedicated to unionism and Protestantism, and the emergence of nationalist groupings committed to achieving an independent Irish republic through armed struggle.

Yet the Act of Union was intended to heal and manage these divisions. Great Britain and Ireland now became a single, renamed polity: the United Kingdom of Great Britain and Ireland. The cross of St Patrick joined the crosses of St George and St Andrew on the Union flag. The Protestant-monopolised Dublin parliament was abolished, and Ireland received direct representation at Westminster, places in the House of Lords and a hundred seats in the House of Commons. The avowed official intention was also to settle what one politician styled a 'hereditary feud existing between two nations on the same land'.

Now formally amalgamated with Britain, it was argued, Ireland's Protestant minority would feel more secure, and consequently religious animosities would begin to fade, especially as Ireland's Catholics were also to be conciliated. The initial versions of the Act of Union admitted them to civil rights on the same basis as Protestants. This proved a concession too far to powerful vested interests, not least to George III. He is often described as the king who lost

America. He can with more justice be viewed as the monarch who helped to sabotage a moderately enlightened settlement with Ireland. Catholics throughout the UK did win emancipation in 1829, but this came about as a result of renewed agitation in Ireland, not as a concomitant of union that might have rendered it more acceptable.

You might think all this would doom the Act of Union. You might certainly think so in the light of the Great Famine, which – through death and enforced emigration – cut Ireland's population from 8.5 million in 1846 to 6.5 million five years later. Yet despite this catastrophe, which called into question the degree to which Irishmen and women really were regarded as *fellow* subjects, Ireland and Great Britain continued to be closely interlinked and even interdependent.

Varieties of Irish were indispensable to the Union state. By 1830, the so-called British army contained more Irish than English troops; even at the start of the twentieth century, Irishmen still made up 13 per cent of the army. The Irish were also integral actors in the empire, both as administrators and as colonists, and empire's multiple opportunities helped to render the Union rather more palatable. Irish Catholic priests, for instance, were sometimes markedly enthusiastic advocates of overseas British expansion, because of the opportunities it afforded to make converts worldwide. In addition, growing numbers of Irish came to Britain itself. There were almost 800,000 of them living there by 1881, which helps to explain why some 6 million people in Great Britain now claim Irish ancestry.

With good reason, we usually think of nineteenth-century

Irish immigrants mainly as impoverished slum dwellers, or perhaps as navvies working on railways and canals – something that large numbers of Irish emigrants also did in the United States, Canada and Australia. But there were also middle-class and propertied Irish emigrants to Britain, many of whom became firmly entrenched in the professions, law, medicine, journalism, the arts and politics. Anthony Trollope's Palliser novels feature one such Irish professional on the make, Phineas Finn, a Catholic Member of Parliament, who is shown socialising in London's political salons and in assorted country houses before finally returning to Ireland equipped with a comfortable sinecure. Phineas Finn had many real-life Irish counterparts, a point dryly acknowledged by one of their number, George Bernard Shaw, playwright, Fabian socialist and co-founder of the London School of Economics. 'England had conquered Ireland', he wrote, 'so there was nothing for it but to come over and conquer England.'

These connections between peoples, ideas and aspirations on both sides of the Irish Sea help to explain why – from the 1870s to the First World War – repeated attempts were made to abandon the Act of Union, yes, but also to replace it with a new constitutional relationship between Ireland and Britain. This was the campaign for Irish home rule, and its two most charismatic protagonists reveal how intermingled British and Irish experiences could sometimes be. On the British side there was William Gladstone, four times prime minister and leader of the Liberal Party, a man of Scottish parentage who was brought up in Liverpool, a city with close links to Ireland. Gladstone's Irish counterpart was Charles Stewart Parnell, a landowner from County Wicklow of mixed Irish Protestant and American parentage, whose family also possessed English ancestors, who was educated at Cambridge and who enjoyed playing cricket.

At the heart of all home-rule projects was some kind of negotiated compromise. Ireland was to remain within the British Empire and under the Crown. But instead of being governed from Dublin by a viceroy and by a London-based legislature, Ireland would have its own parliament overseeing all domestic business; and these measures would be accompanied by social, economic and religious reforms. Such a package came quite close to succeeding. In 1893, a Home Rule Bill sponsored by Gladstone passed the House of Commons, only to be defeated in the Lords; but in 1914 – by which time the landed system in Ireland had been thoroughly reformed – an act providing for Irish home rule passed both Houses of Parliament. It was not, alas, the best of years to begin reconstructing the United Kingdom's constitution. Irish home rule was put on hold for the duration of the war, and in 1916 the Easter Rising took place in Dublin.

You might think this marked the end of attempted acts of union. It did not.

The failure for so long to reach an imaginative and sophisticated home rule compromise had been accompanied by the consolidation of more extreme positions. On the one hand, many Ulster Protestants – and many of their sympathisers in England and Scotland – had feared that a home-rule solution would weaken links with Great Britain

Gerald Leslie Brockhurst, *A Galway Peasant*, 1920 (© Richard Woodward): an ambivalent image of an ambivalent political relationship. This etching evolved from sketches made by Brockhurst in Ireland in 1916 when he was possibly working as a British spy. But, as it suggests, his politics remain uncertain.

and lead to an Irish legislature dominated by Catholics. On the other hand, from the late nineteenth century, Irish nationalism became more revolutionary, and more assertively Catholic and Gaelic. In the Easter Rising of 1916, the rebels occupying Dublin's General Post Office sang 'A Soldier's Song', composed some nine years earlier. A powerful marching song, this called on the 'Sons of the Gael' to rally against 'the Saxon foe'. 'A Soldier's Song' became the national anthem of the new Irish Free State created in 1922.

In many ways, this new state, which evolved into the Republic of Ireland, was an impressive achievement, a democracy that has endured. But its 1937 constitution proved another compromised act of union. It laid claim to 'the whole island of Ireland'. It also declared that Gaelic was Ireland's national language and that Catholicism was its national religion. However formulaic, these provisions were unlikely to reassure or reclaim the six Protestant-dominated, English-speaking northern counties of Ireland which in 1922 had determined to remain within the United Kingdom. Only in recent decades has it come to be more widely accepted that acts of union of any kind may be too crude instruments in regard to Ireland, and that what is needed are messier, more variegated and more pragmatic political solutions. This work of compromise remains in progress.

# Part III

# CONTEXTS

An advertisement by the British manufacturers of Pears soap in *Harper's Weekly*, 1898, suggests both the vogue for Anglo-American reunion ideas at this time and the racism that sometimes underpinned them.

# 11

# TRANSATLANTIC

So far I have been looking at the different parts of the British Isles, and at the connections forged in the past between them. How, in some cases, these connections have endured, and how, elsewhere, linkages became – or are becoming – sharply contested, or have snapped completely. But the ways in which people in these islands have responded to the questions 'Who am I?' 'Who are *we*?' have been shaped by more than local and domestic circumstances. Overseas developments and reactions to them have also influenced the Union, sometimes violently so.

A conspicuous example is the first break-up of Britain: the American Revolution. This began formally in 1776, and ended – or so the conventional story goes – in 1783, when London grudgingly accepted the independence of the United States of America. Except it was not that clear-cut.

The Thirteen Colonies, as they were called – which ranged from Virginia, settled in 1607, to Georgia founded in 1733 – were much more than distant 'possessions'. In the 1600s, some 400,000 people from these islands, most of them from England, crossed the Atlantic, many of them settling in mainland America. During the eighteenth century, emigration from all parts of the British Isles ran much higher. Between 1760 and 1775 alone, over 100,000 men and women are estimated to have left these shores for America. To many Britons, the Thirteen Colonies – though 3000 miles of ocean away – were nonetheless bound up with their own experience and identities. American colonists were 'our own people, our brethren'.

American resistance after 1776 and ultimate violent separation was therefore a kind of amputation from the British body politic that has arguably never completely healed over. I want to examine some of the responses to this mutilation, beginning with a man who is now barely remembered, Thomas Pownall, and ending with someone who is unlikely ever to be forgotten, Winston Spencer Churchill.

Pownall (1722–1805) was born and grew up in Lincoln, a circumstance that may be significant. Over half of the Puritans who took part in the first Great Migration across the Atlantic between 1620 and 1640 had come from this region of England: the Fenlands and East Anglia. Pownall soon established his own links with the Thirteen Colonies, crossing the Atlantic in the early 1750s, visiting Virginia, Pennsylvania, Maryland, New Jersey, New York and New England, forging lasting friendships with influential colonists such as Benjamin Franklin, serving for three years as Governor of Massachusetts, and reputedly enjoying a succession of close relationships with female colonists.

So, when he returned to London in the 1760s and

became an MP, Pownall was in a very different position from most British politicians. He had seen for himself – sometimes intimately – the ways in which Britain's American colonists resembled Britons at home: not just speaking English in the main, and owing allegiance to the same king, but wearing similar clothes, reading similar books and newspapers, cherishing similar political ideals and consumer goods, and opting overwhelmingly for modes of Protestantism. Pownall had also been made vividly aware, however, of the ways in which the colonists were becoming different people, and of the weaknesses of Britain's authority over them.

Finding some way to address this became Pownall's lifelong mission. His favourite solution, which he set out in parliamentary speeches and in a number of (impenetrably written) books, was for the American colonies to have their own parliamentary seats at Westminster. The colonies were not 'mere appendages', he insisted, but 'ought … to be united to the [British] realm'. This, he accepted, would involve Britons at home having to change as well as the people across the Atlantic. Great Britain would have to cease being a 'mere kingdom of this isle', and modify its domestic government and attitudes so as to become 'a grand marine dominion', a polity straddling an ocean.

However challenging these transformations, Pownall viewed them as indispensable. Like some of his contemporaries, he recognised that the enormous size of the American continent, and the rate at which its settler population was multiplying, made it probable that in due course it would itself evolve into a mighty empire. Much better, then, for Britain boldly to convert itself into a new kind of transatlantic realm, than allow a separate and rival American empire to emerge in the future. Towards the end of his life, Pownall even contemplated a kind of Atlantic federation, providing for common defence and a common market, and including not only Britain and the now United States, but also Latin America.

Such ideas – of some kind of *formal* British–American federation and merger – have never gone away. Nor, since 1776, have they ever come close to succeeding. The failure of Pownall's own pre-revolutionary schemes is usually put down to opposition from the American colonists and to the tyrannies of distance. How could there plausibly be MPs representing America sitting in the Westminster Parliament when – in the eighteenth century – it took six weeks for a sailing ship to cross the Atlantic?

But advocates of a British–American federation have also always faced resistance here, in these islands. Whereas some English, Irish, Welsh and Scots have always chosen, since the 1600s, to see America in terms of similarities and commonalities, others – for a variety of reasons – have viewed it essentially in terms of difference, as the Other.

For many nineteenth-century British conservatives, for instance (unlike some of their successors today), the United States was the antithesis of what they most cherished at home. It was a republic, not a monarchy. It had no aristocracy or state church. Its democracy was wide, and its constitution – unlike Britain's – was written down. Even to Victorians who were not conservative, the US could appear a brash, provincial, sometimes corrupt polity, which enjoyed boasting of its superior freedoms while maintaining black slavery in the South. By the same token, British intellectuals who visited Victorian America expecting to find a clean and virtuous New World were sometimes deeply disillusioned. When US entrepreneurs pirated his books, Charles Dickens retaliated in his novel *Martin Chuzzlewit* (1844) by accusing Americans of hypocrisy, conceit and spitting on the floor.

For others, though, it was the United States' very differences, real and imagined, that constituted its fundamental attraction. This was true of many British radicals and outsiders; and it was true in spades of Irish dissidents, especially in the wake of the Great Famine. Arthur Conan Doyle, creator of Sherlock Holmes, was an ardent supporter of a transatlantic imperial federation. But for his Irish Catholic father, Charles Doyle – as for many Irish nationalists since – what was precious about the US was that it had successfully challenged the British Empire, and that it seemed to offer at least some Irish immigrants the prospect of a transformed life. An amateur artist, Charles Doyle once drew a pair of contrasting pictures, one showing a bedraggled peasant and captioned 'What an Irishman ... is always believed to be under British rule', the other of a smartly dressed individual and titled 'What the Irishman certainly is under American rule'.

As this suggests, when people from these islands have looked at America, what has often been uppermost in their minds has been their perceptions of the situation here, in the British Isles, and this brings me to Winston Churchill.

Churchill, famously, was Anglo-American by birth.

His mother, Jennie Jerome, was an heiress from Brooklyn. Moreover, in 1895, when Churchill first visited the United States, enthusiasm for some kind of British–American federation was running high, in part because Thomas Pownall's predictions were so evidently coming true. By the late nineteenth century the US was no longer economically dependent on Britain, but surging ahead of it in many branches of industry and technology as well as agriculture. It was not only a vast overland empire stretching from sea to shining sea, but on the verge of acquiring overseas colonies: Cuba, the Philippines and Puerto Rico. By contrast, the United Kingdom itself was now coming under pressure, economically and imperially. 'We've got to go into partnership with them [the US]', warned Arthur Conan Doyle in the 1890s, 'or else ... be overshadowed by them.'

Churchill's own initial reactions to the United States were, however, more detached. 'My mind is full of irreconcilable and conflicting facts', he wrote during that first visit in 1895, made when he was not yet twenty-one. The grandson of a duke, he found Americans hospitable but sometimes vulgar. He worried that they were more Britain's rivals than brethren across the sea and, on his return journey, speculated whether, as a soldier, he might one day be called upon to fight them. As late as 1927, Churchill, by then Chancellor of the Exchequer, warned a British cabinet meeting that the United States was a 'fundamentally hostile' power, and that going to war with it was not unthinkable.

It was increasing familiarity with Americans and his reliance on them for literary earnings, but – much more

– Britain's growing neediness, that gradually led Churchill to join the ranks of those wanting a merger between the UK and the US, the 'English-speaking peoples', as he liked to call them.

In the 1930s Churchill wrote and lectured widely on these themes on both sides of the Atlantic. Had a 'great English-speaking combination' been in existence prior to 1914, he speculated on one occasion, the First World War might have been avoided. 'The English-speaking peoples were the authors, then the trustees, and must now become the armed champions' of freedom, he argued in 1939. As is well known, these attitudes on Churchill's part helped to oil and promote the alliance between the UK and the US during the Second World War, an alliance that was bound to become increasingly asymmetrical.

It is less widely recognised that, in Churchill's eyes, Anglo-American wartime unity represented only an essential stage in an advance towards a more durable and thoroughgoing Anglo-American union. The breach made at the American Revolution was to be repaired, and a new transatlantic order would come into being, with a common currency and legal system as well as a common language. There might even, Churchill thought, be something more: a kind of global Anglo-sphere. He set out some of his ideas in a speech at Harvard University in September 1943:

> Throughout all this ordeal and struggle which is characteristic of our age, you will find in the British Commonwealth and Empire good comrades to whom you are united by other ties besides those

Winston Churchill speaking at Harvard, 6 September 1943.

of state policy and public need. To a large extent, they are the ties of blood and history ... This gift of a common tongue is a priceless inheritance, and it may well some day become the foundation of a common citizenship. I like to think of British and Americans moving about freely over each other's wide estates with hardly a sense of being foreigners to one another. But I do not see why we should not try to spread our common language even more widely throughout the globe and, without seeking selfish advantage over any, possess ourselves of this invaluable amenity and birthright ... The empires of the future are the empires of the mind.

This last prediction was acute and far-sighted, but the wider politics behind the speech were not. To Churchill – as to Thomas Pownall centuries before – there seemed no end to the potential of Anglo-American acts of union. The Americans viewed things differently. Less than a year after this Harvard speech, which he himself had helped to arrange, Franklin D. Roosevelt put it bluntly: 'Churchill is old.'

'The Emigrants' by H. K. Browne ['Phiz']: David Copperfield bids farewell to Mr Micawber and fellow lower-deck passengers setting out for Australia.

# 12

# GREATER BRITAINS

In *David Copperfield*, completed in 1850, Charles Dickens has his young, mistreated eponymous hero take lodgings in London with the Micawbers. Mr Micawber, who is loosely modelled on Dickens's own improvident father, is an incorrigible spendthrift and debtor. Mrs Micawber suffers from a no less incorrigible tendency to fall pregnant. Eventually, this expanding family of amiable losers resolves to emigrate to Australia, and Dickens has the couple argue over what obligations, if any, they should retain to their country of origin:

> 'However vigorous the sapling,' said Mrs Micawber, shaking her head, 'I cannot forget the parent-tree; and when our race attains to eminence and fortune, I own I should wish that fortune to flow into the coffers of Britannia.'
>
> 'My dear,' said Mr Micawber, 'Britannia must take her chance. I am bound to say that she has never done much for me, and that I have no particular wish upon the subject.'

'Micawber,' returned Mrs Micawber, 'there you are wrong. You are going out, Micawber, to this distant clime, to strengthen, not to weaken, the connexion between yourself and Albion.'

It is Mrs Micawber who is shown to be correct. Dickens makes all of the characters in this novel who emigrate to Australia prosper there. Martha, a former prostitute, marries; Mr Peggotty and his 'ruined' daughter, Emily, are reconciled; and Mr Mell, a timid and exploited schoolteacher, becomes appreciated and happy. But it is Mr Micawber who is most spectacularly transformed. He is appointed a magistrate in Port Middlebay, an imaginary settlement based on Melbourne. At the end, we see Micawber, now a personage of note, presiding over 'loyal and patriotic toasts' at a Port Middlebay civic banquet. Going out as a colonial settler has made his fortune *and* refurbished his attachment to Britannia.

Dickens wrote *David Copperfield* against a background of accelerating emigration from the United Kingdom. Between 1815 and 1930, some 19 million people left Great Britain and Ireland permanently in order to live in North America, Australia, New Zealand and South Africa. Initially, many of these outgoing men and women chose to voyage to the lost empire of the United States, but gradually this changed. By the first decade of the twentieth century, two-thirds of these outgoers were opting for Britain's existing settlement empire: the Dominions, as they came to be called.

As the scale of emigration escalated, perceptions of its

significance altered. In the seventeenth and eighteenth centuries, emigration was often viewed by those remaining prosperously behind as a way of disposing of society's detritus: thieves, convicts, rebels, orphans, the terminally impoverished. Poor, lost and unemployed men and women were still disproportionately represented among UK emigrants after 1815. But the swelling numbers of voyagers-out increasingly included the prosperous and socially respectable. Two of Dickens's own sons migrated to Australia. As *David Copperfield* demonstrates, emigrants also came to be represented in a more heroic and redemptive light, and potentially as national and imperial assets. 'May we not figure to ourselves', wrote a Conservative MP in 1856, 'scattered thick as stars over the surface of this earth, communities of citizens owning the name of Britons, bound by allegiance to a British sovereign, and uniting heart and hand in maintaining the supremacy of Britain on every shore where her unconquered flag can reach?'

If the millions of English, Welsh, Scottish and Irish men and women settling overseas in the empire *were* to be regarded in this light – as 'communities of citizens' still owning 'the name of Britons' – then what sort of new acts of union would be required in order to sustain their cohesion and allegiance? On what kinds of foundations could Greater Britain, as many commentators chose to call it, durably be constructed?

This term, 'Greater Britain', is suggestive and significant. Historians sometimes associate the empire overwhelmingly with England. But while English institutions, such as the common law, certainly influenced the manner in which much of the empire was run, those moving into this unwieldy, grasping construct as administrators, soldiers, adventurers, missionaries, professionals, salesmen and settlers mirrored the mixed and precociously multicultural nature of the United Kingdom itself. By the end of the nineteenth century, seven of the eight large Indian provinces were headed by Irishmen, while the chief justices of Bengal and Hong Kong were both Welshmen. Emigrants, too, came from every portion of the UK, inevitably taking with them their own specific cultures, accents, politics, religions and prejudices. 'Do not think of Scotland as the little rugged bit of the map that you know,' wrote a Scottish settler in Canada in 1918: 'That is not Scotland. Scotland is wherever a Scotsman goes with his industry, his education, his democratic principles, and his religion.'

Emigrants from the UK were diverse in another respect. Throughout the nineteenth century, a clear majority were male, but this circumstance in itself helped to attract growing numbers of female voyagers. I'm not sure I entirely believe the report of an early, semi-literate female immigrant to New Zealand who 'had a wooden leg, a son of twenty-two, and six children, yet has just been married again! No-one need despair after that I think.' But becoming part of a settler society's precious female minority, whose childbearing was deemed essential for the colony's survival, did allow some women an enhanced sense of importance and sometimes greater bargaining power and room for manoeuvre: 'I like the words imperious maternity much better than imperialism,' wrote a Johannesburg Englishwoman in 1903.

The mixed composition of UK settlers helps to explain why the few attempts made to use 'Greater *England*' as a collective term for the settler empire came to nothing. Some commentators liked the idea of a 'Britannic Confederation'. But it was 'Greater Britain' that stuck; and many colonists seem to have opted for 'British' as their preferred self-description, at least in print. 'We [are] a real and legitimate portion of the British people,' claimed some Tasmanian settlers in the 1820s. By the later nineteenth century, politicians, intellectuals and writers in the UK were increasingly advancing this kind of argument: that settlers overseas were an integral part of the so-called mother country. Greater Britain resembled the United States, argued the historian John Seeley in 1883: it was one 'homogenous people, one in blood, language, religion, and laws, but dispersed over a boundless space'. People still thought of 'Great Britain too much, and Greater Britain too little', Seeley complained, whereas Britons at home needed to view settlement colonies like Canada or Australia in the same way as they did Kent and Cornwall: as integral parts of the self-same unit.

Behind such invocations of 'Greater Britain' lay at once immense confidence about the possibilities of the future, and creeping uncertainties about what it might involve.

At one level, the advance of steam power, which drastically cut travelling times across land and water, and the invention of the telegraph made connecting different parts of the globe together seem far more feasible. By 1876, Britain was linked to all of its settler colonies by an intricate system of undersea telegraph cables. But a developing

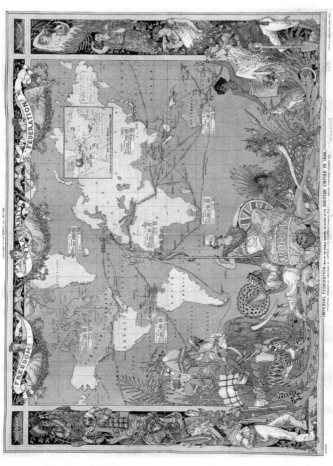

*Imperial Federation Map of the World showing the extent of the British Empire in 1886* by Walter Crane. Crane, a socialist, represents the Empire as connected both by trade routes and the labour of its diverse peoples, and under the banners of freedom, fraternity and federation.

sense that the world was becoming smaller and more interconnected also sharpened awareness of the pace of international competition. By the close of the nineteenth century, there seemed little more 'empty' territory on the face of the globe available for invasion and appropriation. Consequently, predicted Sir Charles Dilke, an ardent imperialist who was also a republican, 'future mastery of the world' was likely to be fought over by the four powers already commanding vast stretches of territory: China, Russia, the United States, and Greater Britain. As Dilke recognised, this analysis presented a major problem. In 1890, when he made this prediction – as now – China, Russia, and the US were all vast land-based powers. But 'Greater Britain' was a construct that was connected only by the sea and by sentiment and imagination.

This was the background to a succession of schemes, devised and discussed from the later nineteenth century to at least the 1950s, 'to federate the Empire by a great act of political reconstruction'. All sorts of proposals and projects were put forward. Some wanted to return to the old idea of giving all or parts of the British Empire direct representation at the Westminster Parliament. Others advocated regular conferences between British and colonial leaders so as to ensure that these men – and of course they all were men – had the opportunity to hammer out a single policy line in an ever more competitive world. But the most ambitious advocates of Greater Britain wanted a new imperial parliament or senate, a 'chief Parliament of the Empire'. This was usually conceived of as an entirely new organisation operating at a higher level than all of the local parliaments of the British Empire, including the one at Westminster. 'The local affairs of Great Britain', argued one activist, 'should have no more place in the Imperial Parliament than have the local affairs of Canada or Australia.' By way of this new imperial senate, the United Kingdom and its settler colonies would at once be cemented together in perpetuity and put governmentally on a par with each other.

The mere prospect of this coming to pass helps to explain why such ambitious schemes never came close to fulfilment. In the late nineteenth and early twentieth centuries – as residually now – British governments wanted to punch above their weight across the world. But they wanted to do this without altering the political status quo at home. As late as 1944, Australia's Labor Prime Minister, John Curtin, proposed a reformed British Empire with permanent machinery for consultation between the UK and its Dominions, sustained by their common ethnic and cultural heritage. Australia was a 'second Britannia in the Antipodes', Curtin urged, and its people were 'trustees for the British way of life'. Winston Churchill cold-shouldered the idea. He had no intention of giving the leaders of the Dominions any more influence over imperial policy than they possessed already.

There were also more enlightened reasons why projected acts of union providing for a Greater Britain came to nothing. Most advocates of a Greater British imperial senate only wanted representation for the so-called 'white' Dominions. Curtin, for instance, was profoundly nervous about the possible scale and consequences of any future Asian immigration into Australia. Those advocates of an imperial senate or parliament who were prepared to consider non-white representatives from India, British colonies in Africa, and the Caribbean, usually wanted them elected on a different basis than white MPs from Australia, Canada, South Africa, New Zealand and the UK itself. The latter countries, it was generally argued, should be allocated representatives in accordance with their population size. Imperial outposts in Asia, the Caribbean, and Africa beyond the Cape were expected to operate by different rules.

In the end, the Second World War revealed both the considerable power of the idea of Greater Britain and some of its internal tensions. It is still sometimes believed that Britain stood alone against Nazi Germany until rescued by the intervention of the United States. But the UK never fought alone. Almost from the outset, it was assisted both by auxiliaries from Continental Europe, and by the British Commonwealth and Empire. Right up to the summer of 1944, there were more Commonwealth troops in the fighting line than Americans. These Commonwealth allies were not just nominally white. Some 2.5 million troops from the Dominions fought with the UK in the Second World War. So, too, did two million Indians, some 700,000 men from African colonies other than South Africa, and 16,000 men and women from the Caribbean. Insofar as notions of a connected Britannic world exerted appeal and influence, those who responded were always diverse.

# 13

# EUROPE

She left London for Luxembourg that 18 October at 4 p.m., feeling not at all nervous. It was not in her nature; and, anyway, as she later remarked: 'I always feel at home the moment I arrive in Luxembourg'. Addressing an eminent audience that evening, she spoke eloquently about how her country, too, was finally experiencing a coming-home:

> Britain ... could not have stood aside from a voluntary association designed to express the principles of Western democracy with a strength appropriate to the challenges of the world today. Nor could any enterprise properly lay claim to the proud name of Europe that did not include Britain. Our size, our contribution to the history, arts and civilisation of Europe would make that impossible. It took the British the whole of the 1950s to realize these simple truths. It took the Six the whole of the 1960s to respond.

These words are from a lecture delivered in Luxembourg by Margaret Thatcher in 1979, some five months into her first term as prime minister. Thatcher's choice of language and expressed opinions on this occasion – her regret that Britain had chosen to stay out of the European coal and steel community established in 1951, her irritation that in the 1960s British applications to join the European Economic Community had twice been vetoed, and her evident relief that, in 1973, the United Kingdom had successfully become a fully fledged member – may seem now somewhat surprising. If so, this is because the markedly up-and-down quality of the UK's relations with the European Union and its predecessors often gets passed over or buried under political passions.

But the politics of the EU are not my concern here. Rather, I want to examine some of the broader assumptions that emerge in this speech by Thatcher: her apparent conviction that Britain was integral to the 'civilisation of Europe', and that it therefore simply could not hold aloof from enterprises appropriate to 'the proud name of Europe'. How important as a source of identity have such ideas about the inescapable European-ness of Britain been in the past? And how far have recent decades witnessed these attitudes coming under pressure in ways that are new?

The British Isles are situated on the outer edge of Europe, and they *are* (multiple) islands 'contradistinguished from [the] Continent', as the *Encyclopaedia Britannica* put it in 1797, a year of war with France. As this remark suggests, geographical separation from Continental Europe has exerted a strong influence on how Britain and (sometimes) Ireland have been imagined by their respective inhabitants, but not invariably so, and not straightforwardly. At intervals, as we've seen, these islands were politically linked to parts of Continental Europe, and ruled by monarchs who viewed their position very much in European terms. And, while the sea *could* deter invasions and operate as a psychological barrier, it was also a highway and a bridge. It was not just money and culture that rendered elite Britons such incorrigible European Grand Tourists in the eighteenth century. Nor was it simply politics that made London such a haven for Continental exiles in the nineteenth. In both cases, the seas around these islands and the easy transport they afforded aided European-wide contacts and exchanges.

Such connections did not, of course, prevent the British state from regularly going to war with particular Continental European powers. But it usually did so only in alliance with other European powers, a point that is underlined by some of the most conspicuous, so-called British victories. The Duke of Marlborough won the Battle of Blenheim in 1704 only because he could draw on Austrian, Dutch and German regiments as well as British troops. The British fought the Battle of Waterloo in 1815 with the help of Russia, Sweden, Austria, Spain, Portugal and other Continental states. Without its Prussian allies, especially, Britain might conceivably have lost. And if – as some historians maintain – Bletchley Park's code-breaking work was the UK's most significant contribution to Allied victory in the Second World War, then this too was something of a

Design for a fan c.1676–c.1689. Figures representing the European powers – including Britain – are shown seated round a table playing cards. The only outsiders in this design are the Pope, the Ottoman Sultan, and the Shah of Persia.

pan-European achievement. It was mathematicians and wireless intercept stations in Poland that first began breaking the Germans' Enigma ciphers in the early 1930s, information that the Poles subsequently and generously passed on to the British and French.

Moreover, while the multiple divisions that have always characterised Europe often resulted in conflict, such hostilities did not preclude a strong sense of the collective superiority and distinctiveness of European civilisation. Until the Second World War, and for some time after, most educated English, Scottish, Welsh and Irish individuals seem to have shared a flattering conviction of the primacy of European culture *of which they were a part*.

For some, religion lay at the root of such ideas. Before 1945 a clear majority of people in Western Europe and in much of Eastern Europe adhered to some form of Christianity. Among privileged and affluent males, confidence in Europe's cultural centrality was often reinforced by familiarity with the Greek and Roman classics and by a widespread fluency in French. In 1818 the American ambassador to London witnessed *lingua franca* in action at his first official dinner in the capital. 'The conversation was nearly all in French,' he reported later: 'This was not only the case when the English addressed the foreigners, but in speaking to each other ... Here, at the house of an English minister of state, French literature, the French language, French topics were all about me.' As the ambassador noted, some of the Englishmen present on this occasion had previously been engaged killing Frenchmen in the Napoleonic Wars. Nonetheless, as he observed, even these formerly bloodthirsty individuals took for granted that certain modes of behaviour and culture were appropriate to *all* European gentlemen, irrespective of their nationality or the vagaries of war and politics.

Such beliefs sometimes fuelled what we would now view as racist arrogance. British military and civilian officials in India, for instance, often referred to themselves as 'European' as a way of underlining their difference from the indigenous majority that was not. In this and in some other respects, the claim sometimes made that Britain's empire served to distract and separate it from 'Europe' is unsound. Engaging in overseas empire was actually one of the many things that the British shared with many other European nations. And when British imperialists encountered their French, Spanish, Portuguese, German, Belgian, Danish, or Dutch counterparts in Africa, Asia, or the Americas, they seem often – despite their rivalry – to have experienced some feeling of kinship, a mutual awareness of being all potentially vulnerable white minorities invading spaces that could appear alien.

But shared cultural references had a much deeper significance than this. Until the rise of the cinema, most – never remotely all, but most – of the cultural information and inspiration that British and Irish men and women derived from countries other than their own came from Continental Europe. To be sure, different parts of these islands have sometimes looked to different parts of the Continent: East Anglia has had strong connections with the Dutch, while Welsh writers and artists have always enjoyed close links with Brittany in France. But, in cultural terms, as in scholarship and science, all parts of Britain and Ireland drew heavily over the centuries on Continental ideas, texts and examples. What could be more distinctively English, it might be thought, than John Constable's evocation of rural Suffolk, 'The Hay Wain' (1821), or the music of Sir Edward Elgar? Well, in both cases, quite a lot. Constable's style of painting and choice of subject matter were heavily influenced by the Dutch landscapes that he saw hanging in many of the country-house interiors he visited in East Anglia. As for Elgar, he was famously unimpressed by most English music, but much influenced by German and French musicians. The first performance in 1899 of the *Enigma Variations* – the piece that made his name – was conducted by a German, Hans Richter.

Even after 1945, what Cyril Connolly styled 'the great marquee of European civilisation in whose yellow light we all grew up and read or wrote or loved or travelled', continued to seem for a while an indispensable and precious shelter. When Ernest Bevin, one-time lorry driver and trade-union organiser turned British Foreign Secretary, drafted a cabinet paper on European federation in 1948, he judged it appropriate to invoke the 'spiritual unity of the West'. Even in 1979, as we've seen, Margaret Thatcher thought it useful to acknowledge the 'civilisation of Europe'. Nonetheless, the Second World War effected major changes, only some of which were peculiar to the UK.

Even though the commercial heft of the European Union is formidable, post-war Europe as a whole has experienced a decline in terms of hard power and global clout.

Given its evident weakness in regard to some regions of the world, and its own increasing cultural and ethnic diversity, invocations of Europe's supreme civilisational distinctiveness have come to seem ever more inappropriate and offensive. Connected by the web and social networks to the entire world, young people especially are now less likely than earlier generations to see Europe as a uniquely exciting place, or as a compelling political cause and ideal. In the late 1940s a Scottish Conservative MP and lawyer, Sir David Maxwell-Fyfe, devoted enormous effort to drafting what became the European Convention on Human Rights. He did so in part because, having acted as prosecutor at the Nuremberg trials, he knew what damage Europeans could inflict on each other, and was eager to help create a new Europe that might work together decently and in peace. Now that much of Europe has been peaceful for almost seventy years, this type of commitment and vision has become scarce. Dangerously so, since protracted European peace is historically a rarity and cannot be taken for granted.

But while relative decline and a measure of apathy and disenchantment are Europe-wide phenomena, rejection of the idea of Europe as a political project has often seemed particularly noisy and explicit in parts of the United Kingdom. As I have been suggesting, it is inappropriate to claim that people in these islands have somehow *always* felt detached from 'Europe'. The level and quality of negativity existing now in *some* areas are relatively recent phenomena.

I'll be touching on some of the reasons behind this later.

But let me end this essay with some questions. Could it be that, at the root of some of the Euroscepticism which seems so evident in parts of these islands, there is actually a more unfocused uncertainty about identity at home? According to some recent surveys, Euroscepticism in the United Kingdom is most rooted in England, and – within that country – it is strongest among those who call themselves English, not British. Can it be entirely a coincidence that the only national grouping in the UK that lacks its own separate parliament or assembly – namely, the English – is also, apparently, the one that is most likely to express alienation from the European Union?

James Gillray, *Fashion before Ease; – or – a good constitution sacrificed for a fantastic form*, 1793: an attack on the new vogue for 'paper constitutions'.

# 14

# CONSTITUTIONS

When George VI died in February 1952, his eldest daughter automatically became Queen Elizabeth II and head of the Commonwealth. Her coronation at Westminster Abbey did not occur till 2 June 1953, so there was plenty of time to plan and prepare. The Queen's coronation gown, designed by Norman Hartnell, absorbed eight months of work, and was embroidered with English roses, Scottish thistles, Welsh leeks, shamrocks for Northern Ireland, and floral emblems of various Commonwealth countries. The coronation also gestured to lost connections. India had become independent in 1947, but the Queen's crown still bore the Koh-i-noor diamond, appropriated from the subcontinent in 1850, while her procession included the Irish state coach, originally built in Dublin, now the capital of an independent republic. The Coronation Oath, too, evoked earlier times. As well as promising to govern her various peoples 'according to their respective laws and customs', the Queen undertook to 'maintain in the United Kingdom the Protestant Reformed Religion', a provision dating from 1689.

On the other side of the Atlantic, they do things differently. An American president-elect takes the Oath of Office wearing a business suit and in the open air, in public. The Oath is administered not by a clergyman, but by a judge; and it is brief and seemingly secular:

> I do solemnly swear (or affirm) that I will faithfully execute the office of President of the United States, and will to the best of my ability, preserve, protect, and defend the Constitution of the United States.

Yet if God is not explicitly invoked in this Oath of Office, something widely viewed as sacred certainly is: namely, the Constitution of the United States.

In *some* respects, the men who drafted this in Philadelphia in 1787 took Britain as their political model. The provision that there should be a US president, a Senate, and a House of Representatives, for instance, mirrored the then three-fold organisation of British government: Monarch, House of Lords, and House of Commons. But the men of 1787 were also innovators, not least in crafting a codified and ratified constitution, one written down – at least in theory – in a single document that everyone could read. This invention quickly went global. By the end of the nineteenth century, most states in Europe and the Americas as well as in parts of Asia, Africa and the Pacific world possessed written constitutions. Today, nearly 200 countries do so. With only one major exception, no polity has achieved what passes for full democracy without also generating some kind of written constitution. That exception is, of course, the United Kingdom, which has not possessed anything approaching a codified constitution since the 1650s.

So these are further indispensable international contexts for exploring how varieties of Britons have perceived themselves and their state. The absence of a British written constitution has become so familiar that it is often taken for granted, or treated as a subject for self-congratulation or (increasingly) for mockery. Yet, how did this now eccentric situation come about, and what does it reveal about identities, mythologies and civic belonging in these islands?

During the civil wars of the seventeenth century, the English especially were pioneer constitution writers. In 1647, a radical group, the Levellers, drafted an 'Agreement of the People', an attempt to impose on Parliament a document providing for the 'common right and freedom'. And in 1653, a written constitution was even briefly implemented, the Instrument of Government, which provided for a republican Commonwealth of England, Wales, Scotland and Ireland. These early links with civil war and republicanism meant, however, that constitutional experimentation came to be regarded – especially among powerful and propertied Britons – with deep suspicion. And the fact that it was American revolutionaries, people who had fought against Britain and won, who ultimately generated the first successful written constitution, only made the device appear even more suspect among many of the British political class.

One manifestation of this suspicion was the emergence in the 1780s of a new phrase, 'paper constitution', which was regularly deployed in the British media and Parliament to ridicule written constitutions right up to the twentieth century. 'Paper constitution' proved a useful put-down because it suggested that these new-style constitutions were at once overly intellectual and intrinsically fragile. Paper constitutions were like paper money, remarked the great Victorian historian, Lord Macaulay: trashy substitutes for real gold.

For a time, such condescension seemed justified by events. Many early written constitutions were short lived; even the American version almost came to grief in the Civil War of the 1860s. By contrast, Britain's political system seemed to provide both for world power and for remarkable stability. The graphic artist James Gillray pointed up the moral in a cartoon in the 1790s. He showed Tom Paine, the great radical activist from Norfolk who championed written constitutions, trying to constrict the buxom figure of Britannia in fancy French-designed corsets, garments which at that time were often padded with paper. Britannia, however, clings for safety to an oak tree, an emblem of slow organic growth; in other words, the unwritten British constitution as its apologists envisioned it.

This Gillray image suggests one of the ways in which the absence of a written constitution has functioned as a marker of British identity. Whereas a growing number of states across the world have used written constitutions, not just to aid government, but also to proclaim and communicate an idea of themselves, in the case of the United Kingdom it is the *lack* of a written constitution that has come to serve a distinguishing and celebratory function. Other countries, it is implied, need their political systems written down in a single document. The British do not, and that is part of what makes them special.

However chauvinistic, such notions possess a long religious and intellectual ancestry. The idea that unwritten, innate laws are superior to written laws goes back to some classical texts and was reinforced by the Bible. Christ's message, St Paul tells the Corinthians, is 'written not with ink, but with the spirit of the living God, not in tables of stone, but in fleshy tables of the heart'. British and Irish defenders of an unwritten constitution have often made similar, quasi-mystical claims. Edmund Burke did so, when he suggested that there was no need to translate Magna Carta out of the original Latin, because people here instinctively understood it. It was in their hearts. James Bryce, a brilliant Scots-Irish academic, politician and jurist advanced similar, semi-mystical claims in an influential book published in 1905. He suggested that, while the British constitution could not 'be expressed in the stiff phrases of a code', a 'sense' of its content evolved naturally among those who operated it. 'This kind of constitution lives by what is called its spirit', Bryce insisted: 'The letter killeth, but the spirit giveth life', again, a quotation from Corinthians.

More practically and with some force, supporters have often argued that its lack of a rigid, codified constitution allows Britain's political system and legislation to change with the times, rapidly if need be. 'The powers of the supreme democratic legislature [of the United Kingdom] are limited by no paper constitution,' argued a late nineteenth-century Scottish journalist. Westminster depended

A FRENCH LESSON.

Britannia. "IS *THAT* THE SORT OF THING YOU WANT, YOU LITTLE IDIOT?"

A *Punch* cartoon published in London during the Paris Commune of 1871 shows a massively powerful Britannia warning a British worker that political experimentation is bound to end in violence and instability.

only on 'the voice of the people', he went on, and was therefore free to modify how the United Kingdom was run in accordance with the changing needs and aspirations of its people.

The most powerful argument, though, was always success. As with the monarchy, the existing constitutional order has survived here in large part because – in Britain, though not in Ireland – there have been no major revolutions since the seventeenth century, and no successful foreign invasions either. Instead, at the end of the Second World War, London still claimed authority over a quarter of the globe. This combination of rare domestic stability and conspicuous overseas dominion served for a long time to legitimise the existing constitutional system, and to burnish the reputation of Britain's governing classes.

The flattering notion that the British were master designers of good government helps to account for an apparent paradox. Although Britain has no written constitution, British lawyers, civil servants and diplomats have been conspicuously active in writing constitutions for other countries. Sometimes, this has been done through indirect influence, as happened with British interventions in the Ottoman constitution in 1876. Very often, London-based officials drafted constitutions for British colonies. There were about seventy such colonial constitutions in existence by 1951, and London drafted many more subsequently. And, sometimes, the British – like the Americans – have helped to forge new constitutions for defeated peoples. This happened in Germany after 1945, and more recently – and far less successfully – in Iraq.

It might be thought that for British actors to be so busy writing constitutions for other countries, but not for the United Kingdom itself, would have seemed an inconsistency too far, yet in practice this has not been the case. Rather, the fact that so many countries across the globe have wanted, or been prepared or obliged to allow London to assist in designing their political systems helped to strengthen the idea that the United Kingdom itself was governed by experts and already enjoyed at home an ideal constitutional system. As a British politician calmly told an audience in Malta in the 1960s, after signing off on yet another colonial constitution: 'We in Britain have no constitution of our own, but we have quite a lot of experience of writing constitutions for other people.'

Such statements relied for their efficacy on immense confidence among members of the British governing class, and on deference – considerable deference for a long time among many imperial peoples, *and* deference at home. As the late Lord Scarman, a distinguished English Law Lord and human rights activist, once remarked: Britain's constitution is not so much unwritten, as hidden amidst a mass of legal precedents and political conventions, and is therefore difficult for anyone except experts to access and understand. In order to function effectively, this system requires that so-called ordinary people have trust in their politicians, judges, lawyers, and civil servants to know what the British constitution actually is, and to implement it correctly. Citizens in the UK cannot purchase a copy of the British constitution in a bookshop, or call it up online, or borrow it from a library, and check out its content for themselves.

James Bryce made this point back in 1905. He argued that, whereas 'the average English voter ... knew but little about the legal structure of the government he lived under', the situation in countries with a written constitution could be very different. 'Talk to a Swiss peasant', wrote Bryce: 'Very likely he has a copy of the [Swiss] Federal Constitution at home. He has almost certainly learnt it at school ... It is ... his own. He feels himself a part of the government.'

The fact that written constitutions can potentially make the workings of government more widely accessible and transparent is one of the strongest arguments in their favour. One has to be careful, of course. Camelot does not exist in real life. There is no perfect political system. And even the most distinguished written constitutions can get out of date or work badly: witness the political shenanigans and deadlock in Washington DC during the federal government shutdown in October 2013. But, given that the United Kingdom's government is now so much more complex than in Bryce's day, that its population is much larger and more diverse, and that deference of the sort he took for granted now barely exists, it is worth considering whether a new constitutional order might contribute to addressing some of the fault-lines in these islands. That is part of what I want to discuss in the last chapter.

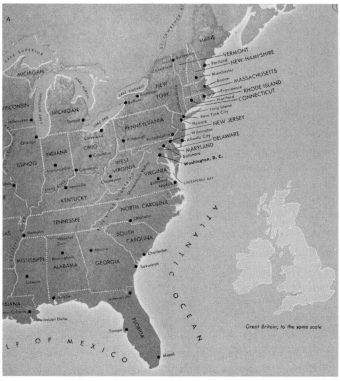

A changing place: A US propaganda map circulated in 1946
in order to weaken Britain's influence in the Middle East. The
image evokes the marked geographical limitations of the UK
without its imperial territories and connections – and suggests
too some of the uncertainties of the Transatlantic alliance.

# 15

# PASTS AND FUTURES

On 18 September 2014, Scots will take part in a referendum on the question: 'Should Scotland be an independent country?' This vote may be a prelude to another, more comprehensive referendum: on whether the United Kingdom – or what remains of it – should withdraw from the European Union. No one yet knows what the result of the Scottish referendum will be. Nor is it possible to predict all the consequences that may ensue if Scotland leaves the UK, or if the UK chooses to sever links with the EU. These are matters of faith, judgment and political choice, not certainty. But it *is* certain, as I have sought to show in this book, that to understand these current divisions and debates (and much else) we need to take careful note of the past. It is history, more than geography, that accounts for the current situation of the United Kingdom.

In terms of its borders and organisation, the UK, as it exists now, is substantially the result of luck, accident and, above all, multiple wars. Each of the acts of union linking England first with Wales, then with Scotland, and finally with Ireland, occurred in wartime or amidst anticipation of war.

Anglo-Norman attempts to conquer Wales began in the eleventh century. But it was fear for the security of Henry VIII's Reformation and of potential foreign interventions against it that helped to drive through the so-called acts of union between England and Wales in 1536 and 1543. During the seventeenth century, there were repeated attempts, on both sides of the border, to forge a closer union between Scotland, and England and Wales. None of these initiatives succeeded, and it required a massive war with Louis XIV of France, and fears for the security of the Protestant succession, to make Westminster embrace a parliamentary union with the Scots in 1707. True to form, it was a still more extensive war with France, and the prospect of invasion by Napoleon's armies, that gave rise to the deeply flawed Act of Union with Ireland in 1800–1801.

The world wars of the last century were no less critical in shaping the United Kingdom, and in different ways. At one level, Irish revolutionaries were able to take advantage of the distractions of the First World War to stage a rising in Dublin in 1916, and proclaim an Irish republic. So began the struggles that split the island of Ireland, leading to the creation of an Irish Free State, as it was then called, and to a distinct unit of six northern Irish counties opting to remain British, part of a now reduced United Kingdom.

But, at many other levels, the two world wars increased the cohesion of the United Kingdom. In both cases, an unprecedented level and scale of conflict aided (some would say over-aided) the organising power and reach of London. In both cases, a majority of men and women in the UK experienced a sense of common purpose and common interests in the face of hostile, external enemies. And, in both cases, mass warfare resulted in victory, and in wider conceptions of citizenship. In February 1918, some eight months before the end of the First World War, the vote was extended to almost all men in the UK, and – for the first time – to some women. As for the Second World War, it gave rise to the Beveridge Report, the foundation document for the introduction post-war of the National Health Service, a huge benefit for the mass of British people in the wake of what was widely seen as a people's war.

It is not wars, but rather periods of protracted peace that have repeatedly presented the most profound threats to union in the UK.

After the Battle of Waterloo in 1815, for instance, no major European war threatened the United Kingdom's existence for almost a hundred years. And it is striking that from the 1860s – after about forty years of substantial peace – demands began to grow for a looser Union, and for home rule in Ireland, Wales, Scotland, and even in England. Agitation for separate parliaments for each of the four countries of the UK, and for other constitutional changes, continued until 1914. The outbreak of the First World War led to most of these demands being shelved, and the period of peace between the end of this conflict and the Second World War was too short and too uneasy for them seriously to revive. Even so, this brief inter-war period witnessed not only the creation of the Irish Free State, but also the foundation in 1925 of Plaid Cymru, the

Welsh National Party, and the emergence in 1934 of the SNP, the Scottish National Party.

Calls for a 'break-up of Britain' surfaced once more in the 1970s, yet again after a marked period of peace. Initially, and understandably, the glow of emerging on the winning side in the Second World War nourished widespread national pride. The existing British order had been sorely tested and seemingly triumphantly vindicated. Unlike many other European states, the UK had not been defeated or invaded. It did not see its Jewish population slaughtered, or some of its own citizens turn collaborators. Apparently, it had won. On paper, the British Empire reached its greatest size ever in 1945, when colonies lost to the Japanese were regained, and additional territorial booty was confiscated from the defeated powers.

But, as we all know, this last imperial hurrah was a gross illusion. The financial, industrial and strategic costs of British participation in the Second World War had been enormous and definitive. Moreover, the deceptive appearance of total victory in 1945 arguably caused Britain's leaders to miss out on a considerable opportunity. Had they been less distracted by the mirage of Britain's continuing existence as a great global power, and intervened more wholeheartedly in the reconstruction of a post-war European community, the British political class might conceivably have crafted it into something closer to their interests and tastes. Instead, what developed into the European Union has proved one of the biggest sources of disunion in post-war British political life, and a cause too of disagreement between the different parts of the United Kingdom.

A changing place: *Vaisakhi Handsworth Park* by Larrie Tiernan, 2007. A Sikh festival in Birmingham, complete with bagpipe players in kilts.

Given its relative decline since 1945, its pre-existing divisions, the end of empire, and incessant disputes over 'Europe', some have argued that the explosion of the United Kingdom into various fragments is a foregone conclusion. And perhaps disintegration will indeed occur. We may begin to find out when Scotland votes this coming September. Meanwhile, I take a rather different approach.

As a historian, I do not believe that major developments and events in the future can be preordained, or are somehow inevitable. The past matters. But, in regard to countries and peoples, the past contains the seeds of many possible futures. As far as the United Kingdom is concerned, fragmentation on the one hand and the maintenance of the status quo on the other are not the only outcomes that may be available in prospect.

As I said at the beginning of this book, every state in the world contains fault-lines, bitter divisions of some kind. As globalisation and migration increase – and they will – states everywhere are likely to become even more diverse, ethnically, politically, culturally, legally and in religious terms. A widely recognised way of managing fault-lines and diversity in states is by improving and revising the quality of governance. So how might this be attempted in the United Kingdom? Let me end by offering three suggestions, the purely private observations of a semi-detached if attentive observer.

First, and as is now widely accepted, the devolution measures of the 1990s were insufficiently thought out. Not only will demands for greater autonomy go on increasing in Wales, Northern Ireland and (obviously) in Scotland, but England also needs its own discrete level of government. The lack of such an organisation – as compared with the Scottish Parliament, the Welsh Assembly, and the Northern Ireland Assembly – fuels resentment, and makes Westminster appear by default an English parliament. By contrast, creating a new, explicitly English parliament, located somewhere in northern England, say, could both provide a useful and popular forum, and help lessen the North–South divide.

Second, if England does join Northern Ireland, Scotland and Wales in gaining its own parliament or assembly, then the United Kingdom will need to work out a more openly federal system. The Westminster Parliament could remain as an arena for determining major cross-border issues such as foreign policy, defence, macro-economic strategy, climate control etc., but a great deal of power, decision making and taxation would have to be devolved to the four national parliaments *and* to local and regional authorities.

There are plenty of historical precedents for such ideas. Indeed, further devolving power away from Westminster and allowing regions and localities more initiative and control would be a return to Victorian governing practice. Between 1870 and 1914, local governments in the United Kingdom raised about half of all the money they spent through local taxation. By the start of the twenty-first century, however, London was often providing over 80 per cent of local government funds, and in the process dictating how this money was used. It is worth considering how much of the current disquiet and disaffection in different parts of the United Kingdom is caused by the over-mighty reach of London, which needed to centralise power in order to fight two world wars, and has not been all that willing since to surrender power back.

Third and lastly, a more federal United Kingdom is likely to need a written constitution, and there may turn out to be limited choice in this regard. Alex Salmond, Scotland's First Minister, is on record as promising any future independent Scotland a 'written constitution protecting not just the liberties for the people but enunciating the rights of the citizen'. If a seceding Scotland does acquire such a document, like most of the rest of the world, will men and women south of the border really be content to continue being governed without one?

A written constitution is not a magic bullet. All depends on its content and implementation and on its regular revision. But, if the Union is to continue, creating one could prove invaluable, for different reasons and across the political spectrum. Eurosceptics, for instance, might well find it reassuring to entrench the distinctive workings of the UK's governments and rights in a codified constitution.

And as well as serving to entrench and communicate citizen rights and the workings of a devolved political system, a new constitution might supply some fresh constitutive stories for a new kind of Union. As we have seen, many of the old sustaining stories and shibboleths – Protestantism, empire, and sagas of the sea – are played out. Inventing a new constitution for a revised Union, with a preamble setting out what this involved and what were its aspirations, would be challenging, but other polities in the

A changing place: Danny Boyle's celebration of the National Health Service, 'the institution which more than any other unites our nation', at the opening ceremony of the London Olympics in 2012.

past have risen to comparable challenges. I am reminded of the words of a shrewd Canadian observer of the United Kingdom at the close of the nineteenth century. He took note of the 'pessimism which sees danger in every new form of political evolution; the repugnance to change in an old country with forms of government more or less fixed'. The United Kingdom is not all that old in fact, but this man's conclusion still seems an apt one: 'A policy of drift will never result in united strength.'

Quite so.

# LIST OF ILLUSTRATIONS

# FURTHER READING

This book draws on many decades of reading on my part. The suggestions given below are aimed primarily at those who are new to these subjects, while including as well some recent works that I have found particularly useful or provocative. It is essential to examine the United Kingdom, its formation, identities and current dilemmas in broad comparative contexts. Recent works that I have found particularly suggestive in this respect are Alfred Stepan, Juan J. Linz, and Yogendra Yadav, *Crafting State-Nations: India and other multinational democracies* (Baltimore: Johns Hopkins University Press, 2011); and by the same authors, 'The rise of "state-nations"', *Journal of Democracy* 21 (2010). Rogers M. Smith's *Stories of Peoplehood: the politics and morals of political membership* (Cambridge University Press, 2003), is invaluable, and his edited volume *Citizenship, borders, and human needs* (Philadelphia: University of Pennsylvania Press, 2011), makes some shrewd remarks about recent UK governments' flabbiness in regard to identity issues. Also interesting are the essays in Daphne Halikiopoulou and Sofia Vasilopoulou (eds.),

*Nationalism and globalisation: conflicting or complementary?* (New York: Routledge, 2011); and Jeffrey Herbst (ed.), *On the fault-line: managing tensions and divisions within societies* (London: Profile Books, 2011), a book which focuses largely on African states, but has wider applicability. For discussion of some earlier important comparative and theoretical works, see the latest edition of my *Britons: Forging the Nation, 1707–1837* (London: Yale University Press, 2009).

Much useful information about the present state of the UK is available free online. The website of the Scottish government, www.scotland.gov.uk/, provides a wealth of information as well as the SNP's official perspectives on the forthcoming Scottish referendum. Reports from the ongoing Silk Commission on further devolution in Wales can be accessed at commissionondevolutioninwales.independent.gov.uk/. But perhaps the best snapshot of a fast-changing UK is provided by the most recent census in 2011, which is available at www.ons.gov.uk/. The online version of the *Oxford Dictionary of National Biography* is not free for general use but is available in many libraries and invaluable. The websites of the National Portrait Gallery in London, the Scottish National Portrait Gallery, the National Portrait Collection of the National Gallery of Ireland, and the National Museum Cardiff contain images of many of the men and women mentioned in this book.

In the categories below, works are generally listed according to the order in which their subjects are discussed in each section of the book.

## Orientation

Denys Hay, 'The use of the term "Great Britain" in the Middle Ages', *Proceedings of the Society of Antiquaries of Scotland* 89 (1955–6); Linda Colley, *Britons: Forging the Nation 1707–1837*, revised edn. (London: Yale University Press, 2009); Hugh F. Kearney, *The British Isles: a history of four nations*, 2nd edn. (Cambridge University Press, 2006); Brendan Bradshaw and John Morrill (eds.), *The British Problem, c.1534–1707: state formation in the Atlantic archipelago* (Basingstoke: Macmillan, 1996); Alexander Grant and Keith J. Stringer (eds.), *Uniting the Kingdom? The making of British history* (London: Routledge, 1995); Raphael Samuel, *Patriotism: the making and unmaking of British national identity*, 3 vols. (London: Routledge, 1989).

## Islands

Academic historians in the UK have been slow to address this topic. But see the following works on specific themes and on island societies elsewhere:

David W. Moore, *The other British Isles* (London: McFarland, 2005); Linda Colley, 'This small island: Britain, size and empire', *Proceedings of the British Academy* 121 (2002).

For islandhood and literature, see:

James Knox Whittet (ed.) *Writers on islands: an anthology* and *One hundred island poems of Great Britain and Ireland* (Cullercoats: Iron Press, 2005 and 2008); Michael Seidel, *Robinson Crusoe: island myths and the novel* (Boston: Twayne, 1991); T. P. Bayliss-Smith et al., *Islands, islanders and the world* (Cambridge

University Press, 1988); Stephen Royle, *A geography of islands: small island insularity* (London: Routledge, 2001).

## Sea

Jonathan Scott, *When the waves ruled Britannia: geography and political identities, 1500–1800* (Cambridge University Press, 2011); Richard Muir, *The coastlines of Britain* (London: Macmillan, 1993); N. A. M. Rodger, *The safeguard of the sea: a naval history of Britain* (London: HarperCollins, 1997) and *The command of the ocean: a naval history of Britain 1649–1815* (London: Allen Lane, 2004); Robert Winder, *Bloody foreigners: the story of immigration to Britain* (London: Little, Brown, 2004; Alexander G. Kemp, *The official history of North Sea oil and gas*, 2 vols. (London: Routledge, 2012).

## Liberty

Quentin Skinner, *Liberty before liberalism* (Cambridge University Press, 1998); Linda Colley, *Taking stock of taking liberties: a personal view* (London: British Library, 2008); Jack P. Greene (ed.), *Exclusionary Empire: English liberty overseas, 1600–1900* (Cambridge University Press, 2010); Peter Linebaugh, *The Magna Carta manifesto: liberties and commons for all* (Berkeley: University of California Press, 2008).

On how – and how far – some originally English icons and languages of liberty crossed into other parts of these islands, see:

Colin Kidd, *Union and unionisms: political thought in Scotland, 1500–2000* (Cambridge University Press, 2008); Gordon

Pentland, *Radicalism, reform, and national identity in Scotland, 1820–1833* (Woodbridge: Boydell Press, 2008); G. H. Jenkins, *Bard of Liberty: the political radicalism of Iolo Morganwg* (Cardiff: University of Wales Press, 2012).

And on anti-liberty:

Patrick Joyce, *The state of freedom: a social history of the British state since 1800* (Cambridge University Press, 2013).

## Monarchy

David Cannadine, 'The context, performance and meaning of a ritual: the British Monarchy and the "invention of tradition", c.1820–1977', in E. Hobsbawm and T. Ranger (eds.), *The invention of tradition* (Cambridge University Press, 1983); Andrzej Olechnowicz (ed.), *The Monarchy and the British nation, 1780 to the present* (Cambridge University Press, 2007); J. Mervyn Jones, *British nationality law and practice* (Oxford: Clarendon Press, 1947); Vernon Bogdanor, *The monarchy and the constitution* (Oxford: Clarendon Press, 1995); Hannah Weiss Muller, 'Bonds of belonging: subjecthood and the British Empire', *Journal of British Studies*, forthcoming in 2014.

## England

R. R. Davies, *The first English empire: power and identities in the British Isles 1093–1343* (Oxford University Press, 2000); Paul Langford, *Englishness identified: manners and character, 1650–1850* (Oxford University Press, 2001); Peter Mandler, *The English national character: the history of an idea from*

*Edmund Burke to Tony Blair* (New Haven: Yale University Press, 2006); Krishan Kumar, *The making of English national identity* (Cambridge University Press, 2003).

Two useful reports on current struggles over Englishness can be downloaded from the website of the Institute for Public Policy Research, www.ippr.org/ – *The dog that finally barked: England as an emerging political community* (2012) and *England and its two unions: the anatomy of a nation and its discontents* (2013).

## North and South

An important starting point is the mapping of the UK's north–south divide carried out by the University of Sheffield's Social and Spatial Inequalities Group: www.sasi.group.shef.ac.uk/maps/nsdivide/. The group's website contains other useful material.

Alan R. H. Baker and Mark Billinge (eds.), *Geographies of England: the north-south divide, material and imagined* (Cambridge University Press, 2004); Helen M. Jewell, *The north-south divide: the origins of northern consciousness in England* (Manchester University Press, 1994); Celina Fox (ed.), *London – world city, 1800–1840* (New Haven: Yale University Press, 1992); P. J. Cain and A. G. Hopkins, *British imperialism 1688–2000*, 2nd edn. (Harlow: Longman, 2002) looks at – among many others things – the impact of London finance capital and Home Counties affluence on the wider world.

## Wales

J. E. Daniel, *Welsh nationalism: what it stands for* (London: Foyles, 1942); John Davies, *A history of Wales* (London: Allen Lane, 1993); Kenneth Morgan, *Wales in British politics, 1868–1922* (Cardiff: University of Wales Press, 1970) and *Rebirth of a nation: Wales, 1880–1980* (Oxford University Press, 1990); Geraint H. Jenkins, *A concise history of Wales* (Cambridge University Press, 2007); Gwyn A. Williams, *Madoc: the making of a myth* (London: Eyre Methuen, 1979); John Kendle, *Federal Britain: a history* (London: Routledge, 1997).

## Scotland

Roger E. Mason (ed.), *Scotland and England 1286–1815* (Edinburgh: John Donald, 1987); John M. MacKenzie and T. M. Devine (eds.), *Scotland and the British Empire* (Oxford University Press, 2011); Christopher A. Whatley, *The Scots and the Union* (Edinburgh University Press, 2006).

For rather differing perspectives on current independence debates, see:

*Scotland and the United Kingdom*, a report of a conference co-sponsored by the British Academy and the Royal Society of Edinburgh, which can be downloaded at www.britac.ac.uk/. Christopher Harvie, *Scotland and nationalism: Scottish society and politics, 1707 to the present*, 4th edn. (London: Routledge, 2004); Tom Gallagher, *The illusion of freedom: Scotland under nationalism* (London: Hurst, 2009); Iain McLean et al., *Scotland's choices: the referendum and what happens afterwards* (Edinburgh University Press, 2013).

## Ireland

Toby Barnard, *The kingdom of Ireland, 1641–1760* (New York: Palgrave Macmillan, 2004); S. J. Connolly, *Religion, law and power: the making of Protestant Ireland, 1660–1760* (Oxford: Clarendon Press, 1992); Paul Bew, *Ireland: the politics of enmity, 1789–2006* (Oxford University Press, 2007); Alvin Jackson, *The two unions: Ireland, Scotland, and the survival of the United Kingdom, 1707–2007* (Oxford University Press, 2012); Marianne Elliott, *When God took sides: religion and identity in Ireland – unfinished history* (Oxford University Press, 2009); James Loughlin, *The British monarchy and Ireland: 1800 to the present* (Cambridge University Press, 2007); Kevin Kenny (ed.), *Ireland and the British Empire* (Oxford University Press, 2004); R. F. Foster, *Paddy & Mr. Punch: connections in Irish and English history* (London: Allen Lane, 1993). Foster has produced many remarkable works on Irish history, but these are wonderfully audacious essays; Charles Townshend, *Easter 1916: the Irish rebellion* (London: Allen Lane, 2005).

## Transatlantic

John A. Schutz, 'Thomas Pownall's proposed Atlantic federation', *Hispanic American Historical Review* 26 (1946) and *Thomas Pownall: British defender of American liberty* (Glendale, CA: A. H. Clark Co., 1951); P. J. Marshall, *Remaking the British Atlantic: the United States and the British Empire after American independence* (Oxford University Press, 2012); Howard Temperley, *Britain and America since independence* (New York: Palgrave Macmillan, 2002); Martin Gilbert, *Churchill and America* (New York: Free Press, 2005); David Dimbleby and David Reynolds, *An ocean apart: the relationship between Britain and America in the twentieth century* (London: Hodder & Stoughton, 1988).

For two sharply different recent assessments of the Transatlantic alliance, see Alex Danchev, *On specialness: essays in Anglo-American relations* (New York: St. Martin's Press, 1998) and Daniel Hannan, *Inventing freedom: how the English-speaking peoples made the modern world* (London: HarperCollins, 2013).

## Greater Britains

The impact of different parts of the one-time British Empire on the UK (and vice versa) is a much contested area of writing and study. For those wanting a guide to the extensive scholarly literature, see Krishan Kumar's 'Empire and metropolis: the impact of the British Empire on British society', which can be downloaded from various websites.

James Belich, *Replenishing the earth: the settler revolution and the rise of the Anglo-world, 1783–1939* (Oxford University Press, 2009); J. R. Seeley, *The Expansion of England*, ed. John Gross (Chicago University Press, 1971); Duncan Bell, *The idea of Greater Britain: empire and the future of world order, 1860–1900* (Princeton University Press, 2007); Mark Lee, 'The story of Greater Britain: what lessons does it teach?', *National Identities* 6 (2004).

## Europe

Stephen Conway, *Britain, Ireland and Continental Europe in the eighteenth century: similarities, connections, identities* (Oxford University Press, 2011).

Partly because of devolution and the growing reach of the EU, more attention is now being devoted to relations between the separate component parts of the UK and the rest of Europe. See, for instance, T. C. Smout (ed.), *Scotland and Europe, 1200–1850* (Edinburgh: John Donald, 1986) and Brian Heffernan (ed.), *Life on the Fringe? Ireland and Europe, 1800–1922* (Dublin: Irish Academic Press, 2012).

Tony Judt, *Postwar: a history of Europe since 1945* (London: Penguin, 2005); Hugo Young, *This blessed plot: Britain and Europe from Churchill to Blair* (London: Macmillan, 1998); David Marquand, *The end of the West: the once and future Europe* (Princeton University Press, 2011).

## Constitutions

Martin Loughlin, *The British Constitution: a very short introduction* (Oxford University Press, 2013); Christopher Hill, *The world turned upside down: radical ideas during the English Revolution* (London: Temple Smith, 1972); M. Mendle (ed.), *The Putney debates of 1647: the army, the Levellers and the English state* (Cambridge University Press, 2001); John Cannon, *Parliamentary reform, 1640–1832* (Cambridge University Press, 1973); Judith Prior, *Constitutions: writing nations, reading difference* (London: Routledge, 2008); Linda Colley, 'Empires of writing: Britain, America and constitutions, 1776–1848', *Law and History*, forthcoming in 2014.

## Pasts and Futures

Tom Nairn, *The break-up of Britain: crisis and neo-nationalism*, was first published in 1977, and it is worth comparing that first edition with the latest, published by Common Ground in Edinburgh in 2003.

Norman Davies, *Vanished kingdoms: the history of half-forgotten Europe* (London: Allen Lane, 2011).

For some very different perspectives on the impact of the Second World War on these islands, see:

Ashley Jackson, *The British Empire and the Second World War* (London: Hambledon Continuum, 2006); Brian Foss, *War paint: art, state and identity in Britain, 1939–1945* (London: Yale University Press, 2007); Sonya Rose, *Which People's War? National identity and citizenship in wartime Britain, 1939–1945* (Oxford University Press, 2004).

For some dramatic post-war changes, see:

Paul Gilroy, *There ain't no black in the Union Jack: the cultural politics of race and nation* (London: Hutchinson, 1987); Andrew McDonald (ed.), *Reinventing Britain: constitutional change under New Labour* (London: Politicos, 2007),

and for some of my own recent thoughts:

'Juncture Interview: Linda Colley', *Juncture* 20 (2013).